Café Con Leche

I DIDN'T KNOW I WAS BLACK

YOE APOLINARIO

Tailor
PUBLISHING

Tailor
Publishing
House

Email: info@yoeapolinario.com

Yoeapolinario.com

Names have been changed for privacy.

Cover Design by German Creative

Cover Photography by Wes Klein

Author headshot by Sheopatra Streeter-Renovales

Edited by Emily Price at The Present Page Editorial Services

ISBN: 979-8-9856848-0-3

This book is dedicated to all the children of the African Diaspora that were made to feel like they had pelo malo, bad hair. Your Black is beautiful.

CHAPTER 1

Afro

A fro-Latinos are people of African descent in Latin America. You may wonder how Africans ended up in Latin America to begin with. Three words: transatlantic slave trade.

As the English brought African slaves to North America to own and force labor upon, so did the Spanish and Portuguese conquistadores. The difference was that the Spanish and Portuguese mainly colonized regions of Latin America. When the United States abolished slavery, Africans were forced to build lives where they were once enslaved. Because most of their culture, native languages, and history had been eradicated from their lineage, Africans had no connection to their homeland. Without a home to return to, they were forced to assimilate into US society. Through many obstacles and with plenty of resilience, they constructed their lives and ultimately their culture in this foreign land—an African-American culture. The fate of the slaves in Latin America was the same, though it was an Afro-Latino culture.

I've always been surrounded by Afro-Latinos. My father, Antonio Apolinario, or Papi, was born in Chocó, Colombia, and raised in Cali, Colombia. These two places are known for their large populations of Afro-Latinos. (Chocó has a staggering 80-percent Afro-Latino population.)

Papi's rich, dark-chocolate hue is distributed over a five-foot-seven frame. His complexion resembles the handsome Tyrese Gibsons and Idris Elbas of the world. Like most Black men "back in the day," he sported a long, oil-soaked Jheri curl. But I've only known him with short, tightly coiled hair collecting at the top of his head. The rest of his hair fades toward the bottom down to his scalp—a typical barbershop selection.

Papi's tight coils mixed with Mami's thick, straight hair produced my bountiful blend of loose and compact ringlets. Both my and my older sister's heads proved troublesome for Mami. Every hair journey began with a lot of tugging, breaking, and chemical straightening. As we grew older, it ended in seas of moisturizing oils and leave-in conditioners.

Papi's rich melanin against a pearly-white smile, along with his smooth-talking, nonchalant demeanor, could swoon any woman nearby. His energy was both intriguing and entrancing. He was a luminous porch light shining in the darkest night that moths couldn't resist. That spell-casting swagger continues to draw in swarms of women to this day.

Growing up, my older sister, Windaly, and I often joked that Papi was the Colombian Don Cheadle. When we saw Cheadle star in the phenomenal film *Hotel Rwanda*, his accent, facial structure, dark-brown complexion screamed "Papi" to our young brains. When either of us saw that Cheadle was starring in his newest film, one alerted the other, "Look! Papi's on TV! Papi's on TV!" Then we would run along to locate Mami, eager to tell her the joke.

Papi and Mami separated not long after I was born. Fortunately, the story isn't theatrical or traumatizing. Spending my weekdays at Mami's house and weekends at Papi's house was the norm. My parents' separation allowed a three-year-old Yorelis, or Yoyi (pronounced *yo-yee*), the opportunity to meet the man who would later become her stepfather, Roberto Gutierrez. Roberto, who was born in Havana, Cuba, has a mocha complexion that's darker than a brown paper bag, but not quite as dark as Idris Elba.

For most of my life, I've witnessed Roberto bounce from baldness to a short fade, but his back-in-the-day hair journey was nowhere near as dull. Since his arrival from Cuba in 1995, Roberto has left no African-American hairstyle untouched. He wore cornrows like those from his childhood but began to embellish them with patterns, beads, and even hair extensions to attain that D'Angelo persona. Other days, he modeled a Sisqó-inspired platinum-blond fade. And we can't forget the nineties staple and my personal favorite, the hi-top fade.

Roberto's childhood, like many Afro-Cubans', was challenging and poverty-stricken. Certain things Americans might deem essential, such as toilet paper or shoes, were often scarce, rationed out, or nonexistent. For a family of ten, a weekly ration of a two-pound bag of rice did not last long. Roberto grew accustomed to a life of little to no resources. In a way, it forced him to be creative. For example, instead of purchasing new shoes, he scavenged for used footwear. Yet even this was scarce, especially for an adolescent with an ever-growing shoe size.

In due course, Roberto acquired a few side hustles to barter with and generate a little income. (Today, Roberto can replace a Honda's radiator, deliver a voluminous Brazilian Blowout, and install a ceramic tile floor to geometric perfection.) He was motivated to take on multiple jobs in different industries, all in a single day. With his jack-of-all-trades work ethic, a divine mix of laid-back yet spontaneous energy, the latest hair trend, and mesmerizing salsa moves, Roberto swept Mami off her feet.

Once Roberto and Mami crossed paths at a Tampa nightclub, history wrote itself. A few years later, Mami married Roberto at an intimate ceremony in Havana, Cuba. Mami, having had Windaly and me during her previous marriage, completed our family with the births of my little sister and brother. When she united with Roberto, Mami had once again merged her life with an Afro-Latino.

I spent countless weekends and summer days at my Tia Mayra's house, causing mischief with my favorite cousin, Dayanara. I fell in love with Roberto's mother, my newest grandmother, Yaya. She was the most spicy-tempered, carefree spirit I had ever encountered. Many of my memories include a five-foot-two, 120-pound, stunning older Black woman being boisterous at a family function, with a Cuban cigar in her left hand and a bottle of Bacardi in her right. Yaya was the life of every party. Roberto's family morphed into mine, becoming no different than my blood relatives on Papi's side.

Roberto practiced Santería, an Afro-Cuban faith introduced by West African slaves and preserved through the decades. Santería became a routine practice in my household: I took part in spiritual baths, cleaning rituals, and prayers to our orisha, Babalú-Aye.

I could recount the characteristics and tales of my favorite orishas, like Oshun, the orisha of love and fertility, and Yemaya, the orisha of the oceans, rivers, and motherhood. Some songs in the faith were also ingrained in my memory. By the time I was ten, I could tell whether someone practiced Santería with one glance, and I could recognize an altar at a family member's home. The religion made its place in my upbringing so much, I have little to no memory of life before it.

The African Diaspora is deeply woven into Latino culture. The flavor of the African tambor, mixed with European and Indigenous sounds, birthed new music. The African pilón, a kitchen tool used to mash ingredients, is a necessary instrument in my family's dinner preparation. Some salsa songs even include African chants that fill the chorus or background layer.

My childhood orbited African culture. African DNA has flowed through my veins since I was conceived. I cannot discuss Latino history in any way, shape, or form without including Afro-Latino history. Africa surrounds me like matter in the air. It always has. For some reason, though, I had no idea I was Black.

CHAPTER 2

Where Did You Take That Monkey From?

A wilda Ivette Renovales, also known as Windy, Windola, or—to my siblings and me—Mami, came into the world on March 26, 1970, in Ponce, Puerto Rico.

She was a perfect seven-pound, nineteen-inch gift to Awilda Vasquez and Luis "Kikin" Renovales, Mita and Papito. Little Windy's beautiful ivory skin contrasted her rich, almost jet-black hair. (When I was a kid, the two opposing colors astounded me. I was absolutely certain that Mami was Snow White.) Her large, dark-brown eyes were striking on her tiny face, which always expressed her latest emotion, and her naturally plump lips were as pink as bubblegum.

She was one of the most beautiful babies Awilda and Kikin had ever seen. Even though Kikin, with his Puerto Rican machismo and Renovales pride, would have preferred a son as his firstborn, he fell in love with baby Windy at first sight. She was equally smitten and, from that moment on, Daddy's little girl.

Baby Windy had a few of Awilda's facial characteristics, but overall, it was as if Kikin spit her out on his own. Almost all her features, from her gorgeous eyes to her plump lips, were due to Renovales genes. Her thick, dark hair screamed Renovales. Out of all Kikin's talents, his ability to grow hair reigns first place. Even today, hair covers my grandfather's cheeks in a full, black beard. It flows from his sideburns, across his jawline, and around his mouth. My mother entered this world with those genes well intact. Physically, little Windy was almost a carbon copy of Luis "Kikin" Renovales. Emotionally, she was a mix of Vasquez stubbornness and Renovales pride, making her more than a handful.

Windy was outspoken from day one. No matter what, she said what was on her mind: the nice, the rude, the blunt, and everything in between. And ten times out of ten, Papito was there to back her up. He supported almost everything little Windy did, and for that, she loved her Papito. It's not that she didn't love Mita, but with Papito she felt an undeniable liberty. He was a Renovales and wore the title with pride every day.

On the small island of Puerto Rico, Renovales was an influential name. They emigrated from Spain in the late 1800s and made their presence known at once. They purchased acres of land in Juana Díaz, a small city outside of Ponce near the southern coast of Puerto Rico. Over the years, different Renovales men enrolled in the island's universities and excelled academically, and they owned horse ranches and several businesses. My grandfather, Papito, even played on the Puerto Rican national baseball team beside Roberto Clemente. The only thing that ever surpassed the wins was their good ole Renovales pride.

These men were infamous for their confident strides, entrancing masculinity, and—according to many women—breathtaking looks.

To Mami, Renovales was more than a last name; it was a symbol of integrity and honor. It was the name of her childhood superhero: her father. He was the king, and she was a princess on the path to becoming a queen.

"Tu eres la hija de Kikin Renovales, y a ti nadie te mandas." *You are the daughter of Kikin Renovales, and no one steers you.*

Wherever her superhero was, Windy was within arm's length. She knew her savior would be there, no matter what. Nothing could separate them—until Mita divorced Papito.

By the time Windy turned eight years old, Mita had grown weary. In Windy's eyes, Papito was perfect—her knight in shining armor. In reality, while he was an amazing father, he turned out to be a disastrous husband. Women always flocked to the masculinity of Kikin Renovales, and he wasn't good at turning them away. Throughout Mita and Kikin's marriage, flirtation and infidelity were reoccurring offenses. At the end of each quarrel, Mita was convinced that she had handled the issue and coped the best way she could.

Eventually, as many women do, she adopted the mentality of "he can do whatever he wants on the streets, but every night he comes home to me." She did all she could to keep her family together. But when she discovered Kikin had a second family twenty-five minutes away, complete with a mistress and a son, Awilda Vasquez had had enough. She threw Kikin out of the house and never looked back. The family would consist of Awilda, Windy, and Awilda's youngest son, Ricky. Kikin had been the breadwinner, but

Awilda didn't care. She would figure out how to generate income.

She picked up work in sewing, cleaning, anything she could do to get by. Despite her efforts, her income was still insufficient. Awilda cooked with whatever groceries she could afford. *Arroz con huevos frito*, rice with fried eggs, became dinner many nights of the week, which drove eight-year-old Windy wild. Windy had already articulated how much she disliked the meal, but Mita never paid her any mind. That's what she could afford, and Ricky seemed to like it just fine.

In fact, it was Ricky's most treasured meal, his first and only request when asked what he wanted for dinner. Thinking Windy would request something unreasonable, Mita seldom asked her daughter what she wanted. And on her most tired days, Mita didn't care what Windy wanted. In the smallest crevice of Mita's heart, she favored the boys of the family, like many Hispanic women of her time did. Her son could do no wrong.

With Kikin out of the picture, no one was present to feed Windy's "A mi nadie me mandas, *nobody can steer me*" mentality. Mita was tired—tired of laboring for little pay. Before this, she had never worked a day in her life. The emotional roller coaster Kikin put her through drained her. She was weary of the carbon copies of Kikin, Windy and Ricky, who were constant reminders of her ex-husband. She was tired of the daily sass coming out of Windy's mouth, but grateful for her son. Ricky was easygoing and quiet, like Mita. Windy, on the other hand, was just like Kikin.

Windy's eight-year-old logic led her to believe that Mita caused Papito to leave. Maybe that was the root of Windy's additional episodes. Whatever the reason, when Papito left, Mita and Windy were like two aggravated bulls released in a desolate arena.

One early evening, Windy and Ricky gathered at the table while Mita finished cooking dinner.

"Mita, que cocinaste?" Windy inquired. *What did you cook?*

Windy always had something to say about dinner. Mita's patience had been thinning day by day, and this time her internal pressure cooker imploded: "Que importa?! Lo que cocine te lo tienes que comer! Y hice arroz con huevos, coño!" *What does it matter?! Whatever I cook, you have to eat it! And I made rice with eggs, damn it!*

Windy's rage overtook her tiny frame. Mita wouldn't dare talk to her like that if Papito was still home. Windy thought that was probably how she drove Papito away in the first place!

Overpowered by her agitation, Windy dashed out the front door, hoisted herself on top of the patio wall, took a deep breath, and wailed, "Ayudame!" *Help me!* "Alguien llame a mi papa! Mi mamá me esta matando de hambre, dándome comida de pobre!" *Someone call my dad! My mom is killing me with hunger! She's feeding us poor people's food!*

She hoped the entire *pueblo* heard her. She hoped that someone had relayed the message and Papito was already on his way to rescue her. With all her might, she hoped that he heard her message because as soon as the cries left her mouth, the palm of her mother's hand stretched across the back of her head, clenched every strand of hair, and yanked her to the floor.

"Mira cojone!" *Look, damn it!* "Tu papá no puede

salvarte! Somos solo tú y yo! Acostúmbrate!" *Your father can't save you! It's just you and me! Get used to it!*

Gripping Windy's hair, Mita dragged the screaming girl from the patio all the way to her bedroom. She threw Windy onto her bed, shut off the light, and slammed the door behind her.

"Cuando termines de portarte mal, puedes venir a comer!" Mita howled from the kitchen. *When you are done misbehaving, you can come eat!*

Windy didn't show until the following day. She decided she'd rather go to sleep hungry than eat another plate of *arroz con huevos*. By midnight, Mita had given up and tucked herself into bed. Exhaustion won the fight, and she had to get some rest before work the next day. If Windy was *really* hungry, Mita thought, she would eat.

The tension between the two lasted through Windy's teenage years. They butted heads on everything from Windy's liberal mouth to her newest fashion choices. Thanks to Papito's teachings, Windy lived with boastful confidence and freedom. Her outgoing, radiant personality captivated many. Making friends was never an issue for her; wherever she went, groups followed.

Her dating life was no different. Mita already had her hands full with Windy, but her frustration reached new heights when her daughter began dating. It wasn't about how many boyfriends Windy had, and she wasn't worried about having a sexually active daughter.

What horrified Mita, in every fiber of her being, was Windy's type. Windy admired most men, but if he was handsome, tall, and chocolate, she was on him like white on rice. She loved Black men. The young Afro-Puertorriqueño,

Afro–Puerto Rican, men had a particular flavor she couldn't resist.

To distance herself from Kikin's drama, Mita moved her family from Juana Díaz to Tampa, Florida. This was before Mita had become aware of Windy's dating preferences. In this new city, fifteen-year-old Windy was exposed to different Black men: Cubans, Dominicans, Panamanians.

Although her English wasn't the best, it didn't stop her from pursuing Black-American men as well. Dropped into this new realm of eye candy, Windy ventured into dating while adapting to life on American soil. Papito, having met some of her exes back on the island, was well aware of Windy's type. The only person who remained in the dark was Mita.

Two years later, a fake ID–toting, seventeen-year-old Windy Renovales—or Juanita Ramirez, according to the ID —entered a nightclub with her closest friends. Dressed in their best outfits, the ladies swayed blissfully across the dance floor to all the hits of 1986.

Windy's moves came to a halt when she noticed a face across the room. It belonged to a handsome, dark-skinned man with soft Jheri curls budding from his roots and resting on his cheekbones. She knew that face! It belonged to an ex in Puerto Rico. What was he doing here? she wondered. How did he end up in Tampa? Windy excused herself from her friends and made her way across the room. When she was halfway there, her clouded nightclub vision cleared up, and the once-familiar face morphed into someone unrecognizable. That wasn't her ex!

Thankful she hadn't reached him yet, Windy swiftly turned around and incorporated a few dance moves to disguise her mistake. She returned to her friends and continued swaying her hips and moving to the beat. She dropped, popped, and locked, but a feeling came over her. Something was off. Someone was watching her. Who? And from what direction? She glanced around the club until her gaze met a set of eyes already fixated on her. They belonged to the handsome man she mistook for her ex.

Windy examined his features. He was more breathtaking than her ex. His cheekbones sat high and led to a chiseled jawline. His eyes were small, almond-shaped, and ever so slightly slanted upward. He looked relaxed and self-assured in his stylish two-piece suit. Did he notice her failed attempt to approach him? Was it awkward? It wasn't intentional. She thought she knew him. She didn't, but after getting a second look, she wanted to.

Windy kept dancing with her friends, glancing up from time to time to ensure his gaze was still on her. A woman, possibly a date, accompanied the handsome stranger that night. But when she excused herself to go to the restroom, he seized the opportunity to approach Windy, introducing himself as Antonio Apolinario and asking if she'd like to dance. Windy accepted. From that moment on, he didn't leave her side. They danced until the nightclub closed its doors.

As soon as Windy and Antonio met, they were inseparable and spent every weekend together. Salsa-dancing the night away was their favorite pastime. Everyone approved of Antonio. Her often-protective little brother, Ricky, was content as long as his sister was happy and treated well. The only person whose eyebrows furrowed at the mere sight of Antonio was Mita.

One Saturday night, Windy made countless back-and-forth trips from the bathroom to her bedroom to prepare for another date night with Antonio. She slipped on an outfit, replaced the shirt, changed the shoes, and then swapped the look altogether. In front of the mirror, she applied the finishing touches on her makeup. As she completed the last stroke of blush, a car horn honked from the street. Windy grabbed her belongings and strolled to the kitchen to say goodbye to Mita.

"Nos vemos ahorita." *I'll see you later.* Windy kissed her mother on the cheek.

"Ten cuidado y quedate con tus amigas," Mita cautioned. *Be careful and stay with your friends.*

One word rang through Windy's ears: "friends." She was going out with her boyfriend, not her friends, just as she had the past couple of weekends. Windy inspected Mita to make sure she wasn't wearing pajamas. Awilda Vasquez wouldn't even go to the mailbox at the end of the driveway without a presentable outfit on.

"Mita, quiero presentarte a alguien." *I want to introduce you to somebody.*

Mita raised her eyebrows. "Quien?"

"Mi novio," Windy said, exhaling nervously. *My boyfriend.*

A stern but calm expression came over Mita's face. She nodded. Relieved, Windy led her mother down the driveway. Antonio looked into the rearview mirror, straightened his collared shirt, and got out of the car. As soon as Mita laid eyes on Antonio, her eyebrows furrowed.

A smiling, clueless Windy held out her hand and said, "Mita, este es..."

"Ay, Windy! De qué zoológico sacastes ese mono?! Que feo!" *What zoo did you take this monkey from?! How ugly!*

Smoke poured from Windy's ears as she screamed in Spanish, "It doesn't matter where I met him! This is my boyfriend and your opinion is not important! And he speaks Spanish, Mita! He's Colombian, and his name is Antonio! You are a racist! Congratulations!"

Before Mita could reply, Windy had grabbed Antonio, packed him into the car, climbed in herself, and drove off, leaving Mita in the driveway.

Silence filled the car until the couple arrived at the night-club, when Windy placed her hand on top of Antonio's. They exchanged a look. Antonio kissed the top of her hand and nodded. Then they danced the night away.

CHAPTER 3

Apolinario-Renovales

indaly Ann Apolinario-Renovales arrived on March 26, 1991, Mami's twenty-first birthday. The name "Windaly" was derived from Mami's child-hood nickname, Windola. Her middle name, Ann, represented Mami's resistance to the name "Antonia" being anywhere near the birth certificate. Not to mention that she liked the sound of "Windaly Ann"; it had an American ring to it. Both Antonio's and her family members begged Mami to name their baby girl Antonia. They said it was perfect. They said it was a beautiful way to honor her husband. She adored Papi, but there was no way she was naming her firstborn "Antonia." Mami compromised: her middle name would be Ann, like the first letters of her husband's name.

Windaly was a serene, well-tempered baby girl. Her face was a light-skinned replica of her father's; she had his slanted, almond-shaped eyes and high cheekbones. Her complexion was neither Mami's nor Papi's, but somewhere in the middle. Windaly's head was full of dark-brown hair that sprouted as straight as sewing needles but curved into a strange cowlick at the ends. Mami recognized the rich, dark-brown pigment and overwhelming thickness of the hair as Renovales staples. She dealt with it every morning before work. The stubborn cowlick that refused to lie down, however, was novel.

In no time, her hair evolved into tight coils curling in every single direction—an Apolinario staple. By her first birthday, Windaly's hair was a thorough mixture of both Mami's and Papi's. Renovales made its Spaniard presence known through its thickness and dark color. Looking back, Mami joked, "A lot of babies are born with no hair or thinner hair that thickens as they get older. Windaly never even gave me a chance to meet her scalp! *Jajaja!*"

While Renovales dictated the amount of hair and its color, Apolinario dictated the texture. Windaly's curls were so compact, they extended three inches when stretched. According to the hair-type chart, hers teetered between 3C and 4A. Mami styled Windaly's hair beautifully for the most part. Understanding the thickness, she gripped it with indescribable strength and brushed it back into two pigtail braids with knockers; a half-up, half-down style; or a high ponytail. Mami refused to permit a strand or lock to be out of place. She pulled with a vengeance first and laid the baby hairs later. Although Windaly's eyes naturally slanted upward, family members teased that her mother's hairstyles were the cause.

Most mixed-race kids from "back in the day"—those raised by a White mother, in particular—recall nothing but horror stories in their hair journey. Many of my mixed friends have an endless supply. If a White momma doesn't take the time to learn about mixed or Black textures, things can get scary real quick. Heck, even some of my mixed friends with Black mommas have hair horror stories!

There is a vast spectrum of Black hair, and different hair textures have different needs. For example, some textures can handle heat better than others. A woman with 4C hair may not fathom how to care for 3C. If a Black woman has only had straight, chemically treated hair, how would she know about natural hair care?

When I was seventeen, I made an appointment at a Black hair salon instead of going to the Dominicans in my neighborhood. I had anxiety about speaking broken Spanish in front of the Dominicans, not to mention that they always wanted to straighten my hair. Perhaps, I thought, the women at a Black hair salon could show me the best products and healthy hair-care techniques. I'd already envisioned myself strutting out of the salon like a new woman.

I never thought I'd end up in a salon chair, eyes wide, watching an older Black woman battle my hair, her hands twisting in all directions in my curls. After scanning the salon, I noticed none of the women wore their natural hair, and it all made sense. How would she know how to do my hair if she didn't regularly deal with the texture? Nowadays, it's common for Black women to wear their natural hair. Natural hairstyles are acceptable in most professional careers, and some cosmetology schools include education on Black hair textures. Over the years, I've even watched the selection of natural-hair products in stores grow from one row to an entire aisle. And for parents out there with mixed-race children, YouTube has hours of tutorials. Hopefully, the days of traumatic hair stories are behind us.

Our upbringing was different. Though Mami's airtight

grip was slightly disturbing, she kept oils and conditioners on standby. Our hair didn't produce that much grease, so washing it once a week would do just fine. She never attempted to untangle dry hair; she'd instead work with small sections and a spray bottle filled with water and conditioner. Natural hair took time to detangle and style, especially on wash days: time to apply a moisturizing product section by section, and time to straighten it out and pray it stood a chance against Florida's humidity.

As the years passed, Mami's work intensified, her family grew, and time was quickly fading. Her decision to chemically straighten our hair with relaxers gifted her more time. I was nine years old; Windaly was thirteen. After the relaxers, we completed our morning routine in half the time. Our hair seldom tangled; three swipes of a hairbrush smoothed any knot in the making, no sectioning off needed. Florida's humidity became a distant enemy, which would resurface as our roots grew out.

Mami may have treated our craniums with damaging relaxers, but her reason was not lack of knowledge—it was lack of time and patience. I won't follow in her footsteps for my future children, but I don't blame Mami. I lose patience with my hair at least once a week! Windaly's hair journey also took some twists and turns, but today she wears her natural hair with pride. And she still looks like a carbon copy of Papi. That hasn't changed.

I may be biased, but five years after Windaly entered this world, the most divine event occurred: Windy was expecting her second child.

As soon as the baby's sex could be identified, the doctor, Windy, and all her family swore she was having a boy. Every ultrasound image displayed her perfect baby, fast asleep, with one hand between his legs while the other hand rested on his mouth. Because his legs were closed in his sweet baby-cradle position, there was no clear image of the genitalia. When the transducer neared the baby's posterior, a tiny shape protruded from the bottom of its thighs. The doctor concluded that the shape was male genitalia and Windy was going to have a boy.

Ecstatic about the news, Windy started dreaming of all the possible baby names. It would be easier to honor Antonio with a boy's name. Maybe Antoine or Anthony? Eventually, she decided to name her baby Anthony Josue Apolinario-Renovales, easily shortened to AJ. Ever since she was a little girl, Windy loved male first and middle names that could become an acronym, like CJ, AJ, or RJ. Anthony Josue was a dream come true. The name honored her husband as well as Anthony, his older son from a previous marriage.

Windy met fifteen-month-old Anthony when she and Antonio started dating. When he had Anthony for the weekend, the three of them spent time together. She took care of him and loved him, and studied Antonio's interactions with him. Every weekend they spent with baby Anthony, Windy developed a clearer picture of what type of father Antonio would be to their future kids. If she gave birth to a little girl, Windy thought, she would already have a big brother to watch and protect her. Windy's heart fluttered with the idea. A few years later, she was pregnant.

They moved back to Tampa when little Windaly was five years old, but Anthony stayed with his mother in Colombia. Windy wanted her baby's name to pay homage to her husband and one of the first babies she fell in love with, Anthony.

Windy couldn't wait to meet her baby boy and become a mom for the second time—until she went into labor on September 12, nine weeks before the due date. Windy's mind raced with the problems a preterm labor can face. With all her might, she prayed for her baby boy, and by God's grace the baby was clear of all medical complications.

Through nothing short of a miracle, she delivered a healthy, six-pound preterm baby, rather large for its age. During the delivery, everything ran like a well-oiled machine. Windy and the infant didn't suffer from a single problem. Still, something did happen to Windy in that delivery room, and that something left her in a complete state of shock.

Once she made the final, exhausting push, the delivery room lit up. She did it! Her baby was here and not just a fantasy in her head.

The doctor smiled from ear to ear and raised the infant. "Congratulations! A handsome baby b—"

His smile softened and his jaw slowly dropped. At once, panic raced through Windy's veins. What's wrong? she thought. Is he not breathing? He's premature; something must be wrong with him!

The doctor's eyes rose from the baby to a worried mother on the bed. Then he laughed so hard his shoulders pulsated.

"Congratulations, Mrs. Renovales!" he announced. "A beautiful baby girl!"

Turns out, the shape the doctor had identified as genitalia was a finger. In the womb, the baby's hand was fixed into a fist and tucked between her legs, with an index finger pointing outward as if the baby was holding up a number one. The doctor thought her index finger was a penis!

Windy froze when the words stunned her ears: baby *girl*. Was she hallucinating? Then the nurse dropped the infant on Windy's chest, halting her thoughts. A baby *girl*. Another baby girl. Her vision focused on the baby and happy tears leaked from her eyes. She was absolutely beautiful. The entire delivery room faded away, leaving Windy and her baby in their own world, gently drifting on soft and magical waves, before time came to yet another screeching halt. What was she going to name her daughter?!

As soon as she and the baby were declared stable, Windy called the one person who always eased her stress, no matter what: Papito. In what must have been a two-minute-long sentence, Windy recalled the soap opera–like event to Papito, ending with an exasperated, "Papito, que voy a hacer?! No tengo ningún nombre de niña!" *Papito, what am I going to do?! I don't have a single girl name!*

"Relájate Windy." A relaxed chuckle left Papito's mouth. "Ponle el nombre que quería darte. Ponle el nombre Yorelis." *Give her the name I wanted to give you. Name her Yorelis.*

The name rang in her ears. Windy had no clue Papito had wished to name her something else. Later on, Mita confirmed Papito's statement. He did, in fact, throw around the name when Windy was born, but Mita became suspicious of it. She was certain Yorelis was one of Kikin's ex-girlfriends, and there was no way he'd slide that by her, so a vengeful Awilda Vasquez decided to name her firstborn after herself. Fast-forward twenty-six years, and Windy's second child was to carry the name: Yorelis "Yoyi" Shantell Apolinario-Renovales, also known as yours truly!

Shantell was the "bilingual" part of her baby's name. According to Windy, it sounded wonderful whether the name was pronounced in Spanish or English. It also had an American flair, perfect for their new life in Tampa.

As I continue introducing Windy's children, you'll notice that each carries the infamous Renovales name. Windy holds her last name in the highest regard. Not only did she keep her last name after marrying my father and my stepfather, but she also attached the name to all four of her children.

Hyphenating the mother's last name is common practice in Latino culture, but that wasn't Windy's reason; instead, she loved the Renovales name and vowed it wouldn't be lost. Her youngest child, my brother RJ, played Little League Baseball in two rotating jerseys: one with Gutierrez, his father's name, spelled out across the back, and another with Renovales, proudly ordered by Windy.

Despite the surprises during birth, Windy was grateful for her "baby girl in blue," a playful term she created because I had to wear blue clothes until I outgrew all the shower gifts.

I was the first little family mystery. For the longest time, I didn't favor Windy, Antonio, or anyone in my family. I was light-skinned with straight, black porcupine hair. My round eyes didn't lean toward big Renovales eyes or slanted, almond-shaped Apolinario, but were somewhere in the middle. My petite button nose was another mystery.

As I became a toddler, Windy noticed a feature that was Renovales for certain: my ears. Large and angled outward, my ears screamed Renovales. But until I was eleven, the rest of my face continued to be a mystery and was unlike anyone else's in the family.

As the years passed, my hair also decided to take on a mind of its own. With a few needle-straight pieces, a few loose coils, and a few tight coils, my hair varied in texture from my sister's. Windaly's tight coils made her hair susceptible to Florida's humidity, but it didn't frizz too much. On the other hand, my hair lost every battle with humidity and frizzed beyond the powers of gravity.

Windaly's skin tone was a deep shade of tan; she was darker than Windy but still lighter than Antonio. My skin was an olive tone, fairer than Windaly's. In our adult years, our skin would become the same honey, light-tan complexion, only differing if one of us spent more time indoors than the other. Hair texture and skin color aside, I still didn't resemble anyone in the family until I was about eleven.

As soon as puberty came around, my features, mannerisms, and even my voice morphed into a replica of one family member: Windaly. Windy never saw it coming. It was as if I went to sleep with one face and woke up with Windaly's face the next morning. To this day, Windaly and I remain "twins by five years apart."

By the age of twenty-six, Windy had been blessed with two beautiful mixed-race daughters, who would be placed in the same category as women like Alicia Keys, Tracee Ellis Ross, and Zoë Kravitz—meaning that people would use the same words to describe those women and her daughters, even though they don't really favor each other. When Windy's third daughter arrived, Spanish-descended Puerto Rican and Afro-Latino mixed in a different way.

CHAPTER 4

Gutierrez-Renovales

M ami almost named her third daughter Tiffany. No one really knows where the name came from, but that was it.

She didn't *love* the name more than life itself, but searching for other options frustrated her to no end. So Tiffany would be the baby girl's name. The father, Roberto Gutierrez—Windy's boyfriend who would later become her husband—approved. The case was closed.

Until one Sunday afternoon at a store when she came across a book of baby names. Intrigued, Windy purchased it, made her way home, put up her swollen feet, and began flipping through the pages. Her search ended when she reached the J section and her gaze froze on the name Jazlyn. Her heart fell a thousand feet. She was head over heels in love.

Jazlyn Chanel Gutierrez-Renovales, or Yayi (pronounced *ya-yee*), was born on October 14, 1998. Whether it rolled off the tongue of an English-speaking person or a Spanish-speaking person, Jazlyn rang beautifully in Mami's ears.

Yayi's American flair came through in Chanel, which is like my middle name, Shantell. Mami adored similar middle names.

From the day Jazlyn was born to the present day, one thing has remained consistent: her spicy attitude. As a baby, she was expressive and filled with bountiful sass. She didn't take mess from anyone. Her feisty personality was so prominent that Roberto's family nicknamed her "Yayi" as a reflection of her grandmother, Yaya, whose disposition was also half spice, half sass. Between Yaya and Windy, Yayi's zesty temperament was inevitable.

Windy's genes were barely sprinkled into Windaly and me. They weren't unrecognizable, but they weren't very bold either. Yayi's features, however, were undeniably similar to Mami's. Yayi had inherited Windy's big, expressive brown eyes, long straight hair, and thick eyebrows. Her nose ended in a small point, another Renovales staple, and her medium-sized lips were the same shape as her mother's. The only part of Yayi that Renovales genes weren't responsible for was her rich, brown skin.

Windy's third mixed child fit into the same category as Yara Shahidi. Her complexion, partnered with her Renovales hair, gave Yayi an overwhelming Indian look, like a star in a Bollywood film. This gave birth to her other nickname: Indua (In-doo-ah). Curious people often questioned whether Yayi's father was from India. Her complexion blew me away, too! How could a Puerto Rican woman and a Cuban man create an Indian-looking child?

Now, as an adult, I'm aware that mixed-race kids fall on a broad spectrum, and I know the differences between race and ethnicity. But back then, the mystery plagued me.

A Black person and a White person can create many guises.

From time to time, Windy reminisced about an alternative name she could've given Yayi: Taína, derived from the indigenous Taíno tribe in the Caribbean. In Windy's eyes, the name Taína was meant for a strong, beautiful brown girl —a direct reflection of the Taíno culture. Based on the appearance of her eldest daughters, however, she was convinced she would never bear a child dark enough to live up to that name. She still holds the name Jazlyn near and dear to her heart, but the irony tickles her to this day. Out of all her girls, the name Taína was the most befitting of Jazlyn!

Windy and her third child were inarguably "shade twins"; they had identical faces with different shades. As Jazlyn grew up, all her features, except for her skin color, continued to mirror Windy's. At around thirteen, though, Yayi's hair texture performed a 180-degree turn. Her once-straight, Indian-like hair transformed into tightly wound 4A/4B coils, unapologetically displaying her African DNA and surpassing the curliness of her sisters' hair. Yayi's hair stunned everyone in the family.

Instead of taking a second to look at Yayi's mother and father, non-Black people often questioned whether Windy permed the girl's hair. By this point, Windaly and I were twenty-one and sixteen years old and were venturing into our natural hair journeys. Although Yayi's curls were tighter than her older sisters', Windy never chemically straightened them. She cared for Yayi's hair with an army of leave-in conditioners and praised her curls.

Not only did puberty cause Yayi's hair texture to teeter closer to Roberto's, but other parts of her physical appearance also started to resemble him. Her petite physique steadily climbed to 5'7". Height was definitely not a Renovales trait. Windy swears she is 5'4", but in reality she barely meets 5'2". Roberto stands at about 5'9". His sisters in Cuba, however, were a different story; they stood at the regal heights of 6'2" and 6'5". The statuesque gene may have bypassed Roberto, but it confidently arrived in Yayi, who surpassed the height of her older sisters.

By 1999, the Apolinario-Gutierrez-Renovales home was boisterous. Windy had given life to three daughters with three unique personalities, and dull moments were few and far between. Roberto meshed well with Windy's life. Not only did he prove to be an award-winning father, but he was a phenomenal stepfather as well. From the day he moved in, he cared for Windaly and me as if we were his. He acted as a male figure and a provider in his girls' lives, all while making sure not to overstep his boundaries.

After her separation from Antonio, Windy had adopted the roles of judge, jury, and executioner. She ran a strict court and kept her *chancleta*, sandal, in close reach. She mastered the infamous "mom glare" to keep her girls well-behaved. Whether we were waiting in line at the bank or riding public transportation, Windy wanted to know we were safe. She was the disciplinarian and vowed to never allow another man in her life to slide into that role.

As her relationship with Roberto blossomed, she kept a hawk-like watch on him. She wanted to know what type of male figure he would be. Would he morph into an overbearing stepfather? Would he assume he'd be the disciplinarian? Would he dare try to mold her household into a patriarchy? Would he treat his daughter differently than the other girls?

She studied his interactions with Windaly and me and compared them to his exchanges with Yayi. Time and time again, Roberto treated all of us with equal love and respect. His voice never rose above speaking volume, except for loud laughter or play. And most importantly, he never attempted to lay a finger on us, not even his biological daughter.

When we misbehaved, he'd step aside and let Windy take the reins. That was their disciplinary dynamic, and it worked for them. Over time, Roberto passed each unannounced assessment, and Windy finally relaxed. Stress subsided. Worry faded away. Her home life leveled out, becoming solid and steady. Roberto was like a superhero, not to mention that she continued to fall head over heels in love with him.

In the beginning, when Windy discovered she was pregnant with Yayi, she wasn't smitten with Roberto. She loved him, of course, but she still wasn't sure if he'd be the one. The relationship was merely drifting in its early stages. Because of past trauma from the breakup with Antonio, Windy rowed her love boat at a slow pace.

When she learned she was expecting, Windy danced around the idea of not telling him and perhaps breaking up with him. After all, she'd only known him for two months, and they'd never discussed children. She worried he wouldn't receive the news well. When he fled from Cuba years ago, Roberto left his son behind, unsure if he'd ever reunite with him. That would be traumatizing for any parent. What if he didn't wish to be a father again? Maybe she was better off ending the relationship, dodging the drama, and being a single mother of three. She'd already done it with two kids; she could tough it out with one more.

Despite the worrisome thoughts, she mustered up the courage to tell him the news. Without the slightest hesitancy, Roberto rushed to her, picked her up, and spun her multiple times. Windy froze during the entire fairy-tale scene. She never expected such a cinematic response. She had known Antonio for nine years when she announced she was pregnant with Anthony Josue (who turned out to be me, Yorelis), yet he said nothing. Instead, he walked into the next room, returned with five hundred dollars, and told her to fix it. This scene with Roberto was the enthusiastic, passionate reaction she anticipated years ago! God had just delayed the scene and delivered it via the most loving, unassuming man.

Fast-forward to a life with one-year-old Yayi, five-year-old me, and ten-year-old Windaly. With every fiber in her being, Windy knew she would spend the rest of her life with this man. She felt so whole in her career, in her journey of motherhood, and in her love life. Roberto, too, felt overwhelming fulfillment. Yet, even with all the love, a small void remained unfilled, tucked deep inside their subconscious. Their home life may have been "full," but it was filled with three little girls.

This might be pushing it, they thought, but should we try again, this time for a baby boy?

* * *

"Wow! Your brother looks just like that boy in *The Karate Kid*!"

"Girl! When you posted that picture of your brother on Instagram, I could've sworn it was Jaden Smith!"

I've heard these statements many times. Somehow, when my brother RJ reached the biological wonder of puberty, his face transformed, but I'll get to that later.

Roberto Jormany Gutierrez-Renovales, or RJ, was born January 9 2002, completing the Apolinario-Renovales-Gutierrez family. Windy and Roberto had a little boy at last, and Windy had another opportunity to use the acronym nicknames she loved.

Like me, RJ didn't resemble either of our parents. As an infant, he was light-skinned and chubby-cheeked with wavy hair and round eyes. Gutierrez DNA peeked through his hair, but no one knew what the texture would become. But as soon as his toddler years came around, his texture undeniably leaned toward his African genetics. Unlike Windy's other children, RJ's hair represented the last type on the curly hair chart: 4C, the tightest curls and coils.

RJ became accustomed to routine hair-braiding appointments and long, detangling-filled wash days. Eventually, the biweekly braiding appointments became too much; twenty-five dollars every two weeks racked up. The braids should have lasted three or four weeks, but RJ had a terrible rapport with durags, which are designed to cradle waves, lock in moisture, and preserve protective styles.

Keeping one on is impossible for a toddler. Before bedtime, Windy would secure it on RJ's head, but the poor durag would have shot across his bedroom by sunrise. No matter what she tried, he was incapable of keeping it on. So, to save money and cease nightly durag battles, Windy cut his hair. Roberto could fade RJ's hair for free.

As soon as he turned three, RJ's complexion deepened into a dark mocha, identical to Roberto's. His other features were a mystery until 2016, when puberty hijacked RJ's body and reconstructed his face into a male version of Yayi and Windy. Now, there were shade triplets in the household. With his manly jaw structure and a curly hi-top fade, RJ somehow resembled Jaden Smith. The first comments rolled in from friends and family members, and if I'm honest, I didn't believe a single word.

Our area of Tampa—Town 'n' Country, or TC—consists of Caribbean Latinos like Cubans, Puerto Ricans, and Dominicans. Most immigrants, after arriving in a new country, tend to seek their own people. Over time, they end up forming saturated hubs of a single ethnicity, such as New York's Spanish Harlem, Chinatown, or Armenian North Hollywood. Someone who hasn't been exposed to multiple ethnicities or races may rely on examples broadcasted through television and media, which can narrow their perspectives.

One summer, my wife, Sheopatra, and I taught a dance workshop in a small, predominantly Caucasian town in South Carolina. In the middle of class, a cute girl with freckles raised her hand and said to her, "Wow, you look like Cardi B!"

We burst into laughter. Sheopatra thanked the young lady and continued with the class. This is a common phenomenon that occurs when people don't regularly interact with other races. It's the "they all look alike to me" effect. As a young girl, I loved the *Charlie's Angels* series. The episodes were action-packed and led by female heroines. After watching the movie, however, I assumed every Asian woman on TV was Lucy Liu. Looking back on grades K–12, I could count my Asian classmates on one hand. The demographics of the schools I attended were often Latino, African American, and Caribbean, with a few Caucasians and an even smaller percentage of Asians.

Like the little girl in South Carolina, some Latinos in TC aren't exposed to African Americans. This lack of exposure isn't always purposeful. Language barriers alone can prevent individuals from branching out.

A community around the corner with mouth-watering Jamaican food and island dialects filling the air can be very comforting to a Jamaican immigrant. TC is full of cuisine from Cuba, Puerto Rico, and the Dominican Republic, as well as all the island dialects.

I've witnessed Latinos swearing that Roberto looks like Will Smith or Usher, but he doesn't. I assumed their lack of exposure to African Americans caused this comparison. So when fellow TC Latinos claimed RJ looked like Jaden Smith, I had doubts—until I heard my African-American friends, co-workers, and even Instagram followers make the same comparison.

RJ's face did, in fact, mirror Jaden's. Still, by the time his sixteenth birthday rolled around, he had become a manlier version of himself, leaving behind the Jaden resemblance. His jawline widened, and more facial hair sprouted from his pores. He and Jaden aren't twins anymore; maybe they're cousins. But he is still a triplet of Yayi and Windy.

After his first big chop, RJ wouldn't see his hair again for a while. Years later, because of busy schedules and unintentionally missed appointments, thick, curly hair ascended from nine-year-old RJ's scalp. He studied it from all angles, exploring every inch with his hands. Infatuated with his new look, he expressed his wish to keep it before his next hair appointment. Roberto respected his wishes and lined up the edges of his son's hair. Weeks passed, and RJ's hair rose to a small Afro, which he often picked out with the help of his father. Every time he walked past a mirror, he paused to make sure his hair was in place. Deformed "hat hair" after baseball games didn't faze him one bit. He loved his hair—or at least, we thought he did.

RJ was the only person in the Apolinario-Gutierrez-Renovales household to ask about chemical hair treatments. Windy made the choice for Windaly and me, and Yayi dodged the chemicals. But RJ actually wanted a chemical treatment.

"I want my hair to touch my head," he explained.

"Que, mijo?" Windy chuckled. *What do you mean, son?*

RJ raised his hand and placed it on the top of his head, allowing his fingers to drape over his forehead. "I want it to touch my forehead and lay down flat. I want it to be like my sisters."

RJ's hair texture didn't allow his curls to fall just yet. It only stood up as an Afro.

The following day, Windy and Roberto applied a texturizer to their son's hair. A texturizer is a chemical treatment similar to a relaxer that loosens the existing curl pattern instead of straightening. Back in the Jheri-curl era, many Black men used texturizers; Antonio and Roberto were avid users. But as that era passed, so did the use of texturizers.

Windy and Roberto followed the directions and performed every step. When the last drop of treatment was rinsed down the drain, they wrapped RJ's hair in a towel and escorted him to a mirror. After unraveling the towel, he studied his hair, and an infectious, ear-to-ear smile overtook his face. Pre-treatment, RJ's wet hair looked almost no different from his dry hair. By touch, it was apparent his hair was wet, but it remained an erect Afro. Post-treatment, RJ's wet hair laid in numerous 3C curls. And the curls outlining the top of his head draped halfway down his forehead. He gently tugged at a curl and extended it to his eye. Blown away, he pulled multiple curls to see how far they reached. RJ must have stood in front of that mirror until his hair air-dried.

From that day on, it was common to spot RJ playing in his hair. Any reflective material was a hair checkpoint, whether it was a mirror, window, or spoon. The family found it hilarious. Watching him that summer was especially tickling. During pool days, RJ shook his head from side to side, whipping his hair across his forehead. He did so *every* time he emerged from the water. Once satisfied, he'd run his fingers through his hair and continue swimming. This slow-motion male *Baywatch* scene sent his sisters into uncontrollable giggles. RJ sported his new curls for a few months until the inevitable day came—he had to cut it. The texturizer left the curl pattern he desired, but the chemicals damaged his hair, creating dry, brittle strands. The damage had also halted his once-fast hair growth. Moisturizing treatments couldn't revive the curls either. So RJ, Roberto, and Windy decided to cut his hair yet again.

The first time RJ treated his hair, I was seventeen. I still lived in Tampa and was wading into my journey of Black discovery. I thought it was strange that he wanted 3C curls, but I didn't give it too much thought. When RJ repeated the pattern years later, it troubled me.

RJ grew his hair out again when he was fourteen, this time to reach a healthy, four-inch, seventies Afro. It fit him so well. On school game days, by rule of the baseball team, he wore his best clothes to class. Perhaps I'm biased, but in his dress shoes, pants, button-up shirt, and kingly Afro, RJ was the most handsome boy in school.

Eventually, he fancied another trend: the revived nineties hi-top fade. He grew his hair out just to cut the sides down! I was shocked but not concerned. The part of his hair journey that rattled me the most was his decision to use another texturizer. He explained his wish to have his hair lay down in loose curls, similar to what it did years ago. To prevent severe damage like last time, Mami researched various texturizers and read customer reviews until she found a mild, supposedly healthier treatment. When she applied it to his hair, his coils loosened to 4A instead of 3C.

At that point, I was twenty-three. I'd been living in Los Angeles for about four years and was neck-deep in my journey of Black discovery. Countless questions piled up in my mind: Why did RJ prefer looser curls? Had anyone made ill comments about his Afro? Did RJ have examples of beautiful, natural 4C hair around him?

There were Afro-Latinos and African Americans in TC at the time, but overall, natural Black hairstyles were still taboo. Most Afro-Latinas were loyal supporters of relaxers and keratin treatments. Men kept a short fade or, like RJ, turned to texturizers. Afros, curly 4A–4C hair, and protective hairstyles were few and far between. Roberto had worn multiple natural hairstyles, but in RJ's lifetime, he'd only witnessed his father with a low cut. Unless there was an unfamiliar school friend, I couldn't name a single Black man with natural 4C hair around RJ.

Instead, chemically straightened hair, loose beach waves, and 3C hair surrounded him. His sisters wielded curls of all shapes and sizes, but they weren't as tight as his. I thought that maybe RJ wouldn't feel the need to change his hair if he witnessed Black people wearing their natural hair with confidence.

CHAPTER 5

Afro-Latino Crap

I've come across the phrase "Afro-Latino crap" a few times. A family member might have said it once. It's shocking to hear how opinionated people are about it.

Some Latinos prefer nothing before the word "Latino." Not White, Black, or Asian—not a single word. They believe additional terms separate the community.

"*Ay Dios!* Why are people saying this Afro-Latino *porquería*? It creates division. We are Latino."

Non-Black Latinos aren't the only ones who feel this way. Even Zoe Saldaña tiptoed around the topic. In February 2021, a Latino Instagram forum posted a ten-page presentation titled "Dominican Independence Day: What to the Afro-Dominican is February 27th?" The slides discussed the holiday and the position of Afro-Dominicans when the country as a whole gained independence. But the reality is that Afro-Dominicans were in different social and economic classes.

The Dominican Independence Day presentation intended to open dialogue on the position of Afro-Dominicans during the country's Independence Day, similar to Frederick Douglass's speech, *What to the Slave is Fourth of July?* Were they really free?

Zoe Saldaña commented, "Maybe just say, 'What to the *Dominican* is the Independence Day,'" even though she's Afro-Latina. Although the post highlighted her ancestry, Zoe felt the need to express her disdain for the term "Afro-Dominican."

African Americans can relate. Our American Independence Day can bring up conflicting emotions. Though the United States gained its independence on July 4, 1776, Black people were still enslaved then. Is it worth celebrating independence if my ancestors were enslaved?

Over the years, Juneteenth, the anniversary of the emancipation of slaves, has gained more popularity. Many celebrate Juneteenth with functions identical to Fourth of July gatherings: fireworks, outdoor activities, beers, and good food. Some people celebrate both holidays, showcasing pride for both of America's milestones. For my wife and me, Juneteenth sits with our hearts the most.

Some communities have celebrated Juneteenth for generations. They even covered it in many public schools before the holiday was mainstream. Then there came a shift: a reboot in national Black pride, relaxer sales reaching record lows, diversity in media becoming a common concern. There were more discussions about Black representation that, this time, dove deeper into light-skin and dark-skin exposure; for example, mixed or light-skinned people tended to be hired more often than dark-skinned people. Hence, a fairer-skinned, easier-to-swallow version of Black people was being presented, furthering the issues at hand.

I'm no expert, but there are probably many reasons why more people started celebrating Juneteenth. A significant number of African Americans have celebrated the holiday for generations. Maybe growing up in a Latino neighborhood hindered my chances of witnessing it. But every year of my adulthood, it feels like the number of Americans embracing and celebrating Juneteenth grows. I love to see it.

Shoot, even many White people opted out of celebrating Fourth of July this year. They don't hate their country, they aren't less proud to be American, and they're aware their ancestors weren't enslaved. But celebrating Juneteenth seems more appropriate. It was a monumental milestone when the United States *actually* became the land of the free.

You may be wondering why I add the words "White," "Black/Afro," and "Indigenous" to "Latino" throughout these pages. I do it for description. "Latino" is an umbrella term. If I wrote "Latina," the description would range from Jessica Alba to Celia Cruz.

If I say Antonio Apolinario, Afro-Colombian, or Windy Renovales, White Puerto Rican of Spanish descent, it paints a clearer picture. That's how we describe subgroups in America: Asian American, Cuban American, Italian American. It shows patriotism without erasing genetic lineage. It reiterates the principles our country was founded on.

The terms "White Latino" or "White Puerto Rican/Colombian/Cuban" perturb some White Latinos. They often jump into defense: "I'm Puerto Rican! I'm not White!" Where does that stem from? This also becomes heightened at the mention of White privilege.

I don't know who needs to read this, but acknowledging White Latinidad or White privilege does not make you less

Latino. It does not label you the oppressor, even if you have colonizer DNA. White privilege doesn't equate with wealth; a poor White Latino can still benefit from White privilege.

Benefitting from White privilege is not a death sentence. It's not a scarlet letter bestowed upon you. It's the opportunity to buy a home without facing loan discrimination based on the color of your skin.

It's the ability to jog in an all-White neighborhood without being considered a threat. It's the media seeing a mass shooter as a "troubled man" instead of a thug.

It's okay to have White privilege. Focus on what to do with it.

CHAPTER 6

How God wants me to be

A wilda Vasquez, Mami's Mita and my grandmother, says she has nothing against Black people. She doesn't see color.

The unfortunate reality is that Awilda Vasquez can be racist. I say this with hesitation; after all, she is my grandmother. However, I can't ignore the story of her referring to my father as a monkey or the questionable statements that leave her mouth today. She has been more than an extraordinary grandmother, showering me with gifts and knickknacks. We bonded through her sewing lessons, a skill she hadn't taught Mami or Windaly. She allowed me to construct all kinds of shirts, bows, and dresses for my teddy bears. And every week, we followed the dramatic twists and turns in our favorite telenovelas, soap operas. Like many doting grandmothers, she filled my belly to the brim with her best cooking every single time I visited. At the age of ten, when I began attending my first dance school, my grandmother covered the costs to help out my mother.

I love my abuela dearly. She took care of me, supported

me, and invested in me, but at the same time, she has some character flaws. In addition to her reservations against Black people, she didn't favor people in general. My Black friends were this, my Cuban friend was that, and my Colombian friend must be a certain way because that's how they are.

The day following Papi's horrible introduction, Mami continued to address Mita's racist comments.

"No soy racista," Mita argued. *I'm not racist.* "No me gusta porque es Colombiano. Sabes que los Colombianos son traficantes de drogas!" *I don't like him because he's Colombian. You know Colombians are drug dealers!*

She had used yet another stereotype to defend herself while ignoring that she called Antonio a monkey.

From a young age, my siblings and I grew accustomed to brushing off Mita's outlandish remarks. She'd blurt out obscenities, and we'd go on with the rest of our day. We rarely shed light on my *abuela*'s offensive statements. If we did, it was when she wasn't present, and we bandaged the moment with humor. We'd laugh about her "crazy" ways and recall the unfiltered statements that escaped her mouth, but the conversations never lasted too long. It wasn't until I became an adult that I understood the severity of her comments.

In-depth discussions about my grandmother's ideals were taboo. Challenging elders is a top offense in Latino households. The only person who was well versed in quarrels with Awilda Vasquez was Windy Renovales, who was now an adult and worn out. She'd spent most of her life disagreeing with her mother, and she was tired. Day-to-day life ran more smoothly if she just let the negativity roll over her and kept moving. The rest of the family adopted the same coping mechanism.

Now, as an adult with more knowledge, living two thousand miles away, I wonder if that coping mechanism proved effective. If we had respectfully challenged Mita in the past, would she feel comfortable announcing her prayer for her first grandson to inherit "good hair" in the present?

When God blessed her with a great-grandson, my handsome nephew, she added to the bigotry with "advice" to the baby's mother, Windaly.

"Ay, Windaly! Ponle un pinche en la nariz, para qué se le afine." *Put a clothespin over the baby's nose so it doesn't grow wide.*

"Windaly, no saques a ese niño al sol, que se pone prieto!" *Don't go out into the sun with the baby, or he'll get darker!*

I wonder if her mindset would've changed if we had spoken up in the nineties. Perhaps it would have, or perhaps nothing would've changed. After all, my grandmother, like many in her generation, abides by the teachings instilled in her as a child.

The love she bestowed on me was authentic and touching, but I often questioned the underlying reasons. Mami, Papi, my siblings, and my stepfather all agreed that Yorelis Shantell was always my grandmother's favorite. It was a truth I never denied; I even found it humorous. But the fact is that Mita's treatment toward me was different.

Did it have something to do with the decaying relationship between my mother and father? In its early years, their relationship was a gorgeous, sunny day, but for many reasons, that sunny day ended in a harsh winter. By the time

I came around in 1995, their love story was cooling off, and Papi was relatively absent. Mami was unprepared for a life with five-year-old Windaly, a baby on the way, and sometimes Antonio. Then the rug slipped out from under Mami's feet when I introduced myself to her nine weeks before the due date. She thanked God for her healthy baby girl, but her mind raced in endless circles about the home she was bringing her baby into.

There was no nursery in their apartment, and Antonio wasn't home enough to set one up. With her wounded pride and head hung low, Mami brought the baby home from the hospital without a crib. That night, she shared the bed with her newborn. During the day, Mami laid the baby in a blanket-filled dresser drawer that was placed on a table. This went on for a couple of days.

Fed up with Papi's lack of support, Mita raided the nearest Babies R Us and purchased the first affordable crib she laid her eyes on. She lugged it back to her daughter's house, set it up, and tucked her granddaughter in as soon as nap time rolled around. As the years went on, my grandmother continued to step into a parental role to help my mom. Papi raised Windaly by Mami's side, but he was distant with me, which forced Mita to raise me alongside Mami. Maybe that's where her favoritism and attachment to me stems from. Or—and I hate that this dares to cross my mind—I wonder if Mita favors me because of my complexion.

Out of all four children, I inherited my mother's European roots the most. My baby hairs curled in soft, loose waves. Windaly's were the cuter, tiny 4A coils. Her relationship with Mita wasn't terrible, but they didn't share the same closeness. RJ and Yayi are as close to our grandmother as the North Pole is to the South. They've always had brief contact, outside of the kiss on the cheek that's culturally required. She's never been as hands-on with them. They didn't spend too much time together, and when they did, Mita always had an uncanny ability to pick the most inconsiderate thought in her head and blurt it out to my younger siblings.

Her comments were all over, from RJ's "unruly" hair to the "hideous" shirt Yayi was wearing. The comments weren't always rude or distasteful, and most of the time, we found humor in them. Many mothers and grandmothers from Mami's and Mita's generations, no matter what color they are, can be loose-lipped: they say whatever they want, whenever they want.

"Honey, why don't you wear a dress instead of *that*?"

"Whew! I love this new boyfriend, so handsome! Your old boyfriend was feo con cojones, *ugly as hell!*"

"Hey! You've been eating a lot."

"Hey! Are you eating enough?"

They mean well but still utter unsavory observations. The difference between most opinionated grandmothers and Mita is balance. Love, understanding, and compassionate parenting balance out the wild opinions. For example, if I got a trendy new hairdo and video-called my mother, she might answer with an immediate, "Nena! Y ese pello?!" *Girl! What is up with that hair?!*

I'd laugh at her boldness and then give her the full description of the style and how much I adore it. She'd laugh, recalling the hair trends around when she was my age, and we'd continue chatting about our days. In fact, by the end of the call, she might even admit the style is cute!

Most mothers voice their opinions to their children. It's almost instinctual. However, it's not intended to cut deep. Regardless of what my mother says about my style or hair, I still feel never-ending love from her. If she was to say something that rubbed me the wrong way, I'm confident we could discuss it. But for Yayi and RJ, Mita rarely balances her comments with love. If someone questioned her judgment, she wouldn't be open to a conversation. Instead, she might explain why her opinion is correct.

Most of my grandmother's bold comments don't concern me. But certain statements she repeats about RJ's hair trouble me.

"Que pasurin!" *What a nappy head!*

"Parece una araña peluda!" *It looks like a hairy spider!*

"Peinate ese pelo, dios mio!" *Comb that hair, my God!*

These phrases often leave her mouth even before a "hello." Most times, she tugs and pulls RJ's hair while announcing her disdain. Why does she dislike RJ's hair so much? Why does his tall, regal Afro disturb her enough to talk about it every time she sees him?

Many Latinos love the skin they're in as well as all the shades the Latino community offers, from ivory to caramel brown and all the chocolate hues. I'm thankful to have known these Latinos the most. On the other end of the spectrum, some Latinos aren't as loving or open. They continue to abide by outdated teachings.

Latino culture, similar to many Black and Brown cultures, model their ideas of beauty after the European standard: lighter skin, straight hair, narrow noses. Anything closer to Whiteness is seen as more attractive. This standard of beauty has dominated Latino media for years. The Sofía Vergaras and Camila Cabellos are considered the standards. There are gorgeous Afro-Latinas in mainstream American culture, like Rosario Dawson and Dascha Polanco, but in my opinion—and I repeat, opinion—Afro-Latino celebrities are almost always outnumbered by their fairer-skinned counterparts. Many of them have more success auditioning for African-American roles instead.

When I was a little girl sitting alongside Mita watching Univision and Telemundo, all the *novelas,* talk shows, and news stations showcased stunning Latina beauties, but never Afro-Latinas. Mainstream media highlighted Afro-Latinos as successful musicians or athletes, never as representations of beauty. The standard extends to a rich Central-American tan, but the train often stops there. It seldom travels to a hue as dark as my father's. Only in my adult years have I seen a shift in people like Amara La Negra and Ozuna breaking through into Latino Hollywood, representing Afro-Latinos with pride. Perhaps now, Latino girls and boys of African descent can see themselves on the screen and know their opportunities are endless.

Although the standard of beauty is broadening, some remain stuck in old-school ideals. My grandmother believes we look more presentable with our hair "controlled." She likes our curls but prefers them flatter and tamed, like when our hair is damp. She suggests using a lot of hairspray and gel so that our hair falls instead of extending out to the sides.

At the age of twenty-two, I cut my hair so that it rested a little past my earlobes. I stopped drenching my hair with gel and hairspray to achieve perfect ringlets. I no longer strived to achieve a flawless curl. Over time, all the harsh products found their resting place in the trash can. With my super-short haircut and nothing but leave-in conditioner and oil, my coils were raised into a large Afro—an actual Angela Davis–esque Afro! I never knew my hair could stand up. Of course, I was half Black, but I had no idea my hair could curl to that extent. I loved it! At first, the inches I had chopped off mortified my mother, but eventually she, too, agreed the style was cute. The rest of my family followed suit—everyone except Mita.

"Dios mío, qué hiciste?" *My God, what did you do?*

I chuckled, having already predicted this response. "Me lo corté." *I cut it.*

Her eyebrows furrowed as she shook her head in disapproval. "Porqué hiciste eso? Te lo dañaste?" *Why did you do that? Did you damage it?*

"No Mita, yo quería contarlo. Para peinarmelo como un Afro." *I wanted to cut it. I wanted an Afro.*

"No puedo creerlo. Te jodistes el pelo." *I can't believe it. You ruined your hair.*

The rest of our time was filled with cordial small talk while my mind replayed her reaction again and again. I wondered why I expected the conversation to go any differently. She's been the same woman since the beginning of time; why would I expect her to like my natural hair now? In the years to come, I would visit my hometown during winter holidays sporting braids, cornrows, and other protective styles, and each time she'd greet me with a blunt "Y esa porqueria en tu cabeza?" *And what is that trash on your head?*

These days, I can't recall the obscenities my grandmother

utters because we haven't spoken in a while. Not only does she have old-school views on racial matters, but her opinions on sexual orientation are just as narrow. So when her "favorite" granddaughter proposed to her African-American girlfriend and announced it on Facebook, Yoyi became "disrespectful" and "an embarrassment to the family."

Given her past, I wasn't surprised. On my last few trips to Tampa, however, the lengths she went to avoid my presence stunned me. Despite that, I paid her a visit. I was determined to walk into her house and speak to her, even if she wouldn't talk. She'll always be my grandmother; she's just stuck in her ways. I still love her and nothing will change that.

When I arrived, I marched past her car up the driveway and knocked on the door. There was no response. I raised my fist to the door and repeated the series of knocks. Still nothing. I could hear the faint sounds of a Spanish radio station, but she always leaves the radio on, even when she's not home. Maybe she left with a friend, I thought. Is that why her car's still in the driveway? In one final attempt, I walked around to her guest bedroom window. It was across from her bedroom, so maybe she'd hear my knocks if she was resting. I knocked on the window three times. Silence. I decided to call her, but after several rings there was still no answer, so I turned around and made my way home.

I opened the door to Roberto talking to my fiancée in the living room. "Weren't you going to Mita's house?" he inquired.

"Yeah, she's not home, though. I'll try again later."

He looked confused. "I talked to her not too long ago. She said she was home. Was her car there?"

"It was. Maybe she was napping or left with a friend or something."

"Let me try to call her real quick." He called her and switched the phone to speaker mode.

After two rings, my grandmother's voice played through the speaker. "Hello?"

"Hola Mita, donde estas?" Roberto asked.

"Aqui en la casa. Porque? Que paso?"

Roberto rotated away from the receiver and let out a chuckle. "No pasó nada. Yoyi está aquí. Ella dijo que fue alla y no abristes la puerta." *Nothing happened. Yoyi's here. She said she went over there and you didn't open the door.*

"No sé por que no la escuché tocar pero estoy aquí," she replied dryly. *I don't know why I didn't hear her knock, but I'm here.*

"Está bien, ella va a volver alla," *Okay, well, she's going back over there.*

There was a brief silence. "Okay..." She paused as if she had more to say. "Okay. Dile que venga sola." *Tell her to come alone.*

Roberto ended the call, and frustration overcame me. "Roberto, she's lying! I knocked three separate times and called her! She ignored me!"

He shook his head and let out a sigh. "She's crazy. You know how she is."

With my patience thinning, I made my way to her house for the second time. When she answered the door, I flashed her a big smile from ear to ear. "Hola Mita!"

"Hola." Her expression did not shift.

I gave her a kiss on the cheek that she did not return, her face remaining still. Whew, this was gonna be tough. If I just start some small talk, I thought as I walked inside, maybe she'll loosen up. I glanced at the miniature town under the Christmas tree. White cotton balls and glitter covered the roofs of the tiny town, and the townspeople scattered throughout were singing carols, plowing snow, or marveling at baby Jesus. My grandmother always goes above and beyond with her decorations. She makes the entire house feel like the North Pole.

"Como estas?" I asked. "Me gustan tus decoraciones de Navidad!" *I like your Christmas decorations!*

"Estoy bien, como Dios me quiere." *I'm well, how God wants me to be.*

What did she mean by "How God wants me to be"? I paused, inhaled deeply, and tried to talk her out of that stale mood, but she never budged. She met each of my attempts with dry one- or two-word responses, which was rare for a woman who could keep me on the phone for days. After two-and-a-half grueling hours, I grabbed my purse, gave her a kiss on the cheek—which yet again she did not return—and went back home. At least I visited her. I tried. But I didn't see her for the rest of my visit. About five months later, I called to wish her a happy Mother's Day. She ignored my call.

CHAPTER 7

I'm not Black. I'm Colombian

A woman was cutting vegetables for dinner when she heard something outside. She stood still and listened: soft sniffles and a slight whimper. An injured animal?

As she walked outside and started down the steps, the sound became more audible. Soft sniffles strengthened into short, hyperventilating breaths. The light whimper was now a full-blown sob. Was someone hurt? When she was halfway down, the woman spotted a small person sitting on the last step, too small.

Once she reached the bottom, the scene became clear: a young Black boy was sitting on the step, holding his legs into his chest, releasing heartbreaking sobs into his knees. What in the world? The woman consoled him until he stopped hyperventilating. When she asked what he was doing outside so late at night, he said he was looking for his mother.

Earlier that day, his mother had sat him at a bus stop and told him to wait for her. Hours passed, the day turned into night, but still she hadn't returned. He had wandered the streets searching for her, and now he was lost. So the woman brought the boy into her home, fed him, bathed him, and dressed him in some of her son's pajamas.

Over the next few days, she and her family contacted law enforcement and local radio stations: "A five-year-old boy named Antonio Bejarano was separated from his family. If this is your child, please contact us." But no one ever came. The boy has been the son of Olga Salcedo-Apolinario and Enrique Apolinario ever since.

* * *

When I asked Papi how he met the woman that adopted him, the story was completely different. When he was seven, he told me, his birth mother sent him to live with his father, Tirzon Bejarano, and his new wife. He enjoyed the home, but his stepmom didn't care for him in the same way she cared for his half siblings.

She neglected and mistreated him while his father paid no attention. Fed up with his home life, Papi ran away and boarded a bus aimed anywhere outside of his town. A few stops later, he arrived in a nearby city. He learned how to earn a little income at the local markets by shopping for customers; he'd walk throughout the market, shop for the requested items, and deliver them in exchange for a few coins. The earnings were just enough for some food.

After a couple of days, a woman named Olga Salcedo, a regular customer, watched him more closely. She noticed that adults never accompanied the little boy, and he was always alone. It also seemed like he wasn't going home after the day was over. Part of her wondered if he even had a home to go to.

One afternoon, she invited him to stay with her. She bathed, clothed, and housed him, all while searching for his family. Days turned into weeks and weeks into months, and still no one had come forward. In the meantime, he acclimated to life with Olga and her children. Not long after, Olga adopted him, making him a permanent member of the family.

After hearing this mind-blowing story, I called my mom and asked if she knew about Papi's childhood.

"That's not the story, Yoyi," she said.

"What do you mean, Mami? I was just on the phone with him for two hours. He met his adoptive mother while working at the grocery store. He was basically the first Instacart!"

"*Yorrrelis*," she interrupted with a heavy accent and a drawn-out rolled *r*. "Señora Olga told me the story when I met her in Colombia. That is not what happened."

My mind was performing loops, twists, and turns. "Why would Papi lie, though?"

"I'm not sure, *mija*, but that is not what his adoptive mother said."

Olga told Mami she found Papi when he was about five, crying outside of her home late one night. I never questioned Papi after hearing the alternative storyline because I believe Olga's narrative is true. Mami wouldn't lie; she has no reason to. Papi does, though. Abandonment would be disheartening for anybody, but I can't imagine the trauma it causes a child. Perhaps the truth brings up memories too painful for

Papi to revisit. I didn't wish to expose the unsealed wounds my father might have.

When Olga adopted him, Papi took the name of her husband. Antonio Bejarano became Antonio Enrique Apolinario. He wouldn't see his birth parents, Carlina and Tirzon Bejarano, again until his mid-twenties. With his new family, he moved out of Chocó, Colombia, and enrolled in a school in Buenaventura. He spent his late teens and early adulthood salsa-dancing through the streets of Cali, Colombia, which many refer to as the "party city."

And in his late twenties, Tampa, Florida, became his home and the place where he'd continue building his family. He adapted to American life, learning English as the years rolled by. He made friends, partied, worked, dated, and met a cute, dark-haired, fair-skinned Puerto Rican woman at a nightclub.

* * *

My uncle Juan Carlos was hollering over the music. My other uncle Miguel stood within spitting distance of him, but that never stopped Juan Carlos from yelling. He was always the loudest person at family parties. Mami and Roberto moved seamlessly together as they salsa-danced to Oscar D'León's "Llorarás." Conversations, domino games, and more dancing occupied the rest of the family at the party. Mita left the party early after she saw the little *amigita*, friend, I invited. Everyone knew that the little *amigita* was actually my girlfriend, Tominique, but they used whatever term made them feel better about it.

Tominique and I sat side by side on the couch as my

living room transformed into a salsa club. After the initial nerve-racking introduction, she had seemed to relax a little more.

"It wasn't so bad, right? Meeting my family?" I rubbed my hand over hers.

"No. Not that bad at all. I mean, it's still weird being around so many people that don't speak English. What if they talk about me in Spanish?"

"Oh!" I chuckled. "You'll know. For some reason, my family still lowers their voices when they talk crap about English-speaking people. And they dart their eyes back and forth to the victim. It's not discreet at all! If they talk about you, you'll definitely know. And I'll be here to translate."

Tominique's shoulders dropped as she exhaled. She wasn't the first African-American significant other to be introduced to my family. Windaly dated Black men before it had ever become a thought in my head, so she broke the ice for me. My family showed no mercy with their comments and unsolicited opinions, like when they announced how ugly they thought her boyfriends were.

"Ayy, Windaly! Que haces con ese negro?" *What are you doing with that Black boy?*

"Dios mio, ese negro es feo!" *My Lord, that Black boy is ugly!*

I wish I could say the White Puerto Rican side of my family were the only ones to spew these distasteful comments, but my Afro-Latino side did just the same. It's crazy what Eurocentrism, self-hatred, and detachment from your own people can do.

I was in the fourth grade when Windaly started dating, light-years away from the birth of my love life. But watching my family's reactions prepared me for what was to come. If they had tons to say about *her* type, then an African-American girlfriend might send them through the roof. Regardless, I couldn't care less. As long as they were respectful to my girlfriend's face, they could say whatever they wanted in her absence.

"You know," Tominique began, "I didn't know you were Black."

"What? Roberto's Cuban! You didn't hear that thick accent?" I laughed.

"I heard it. But he's Black. He's a Black man that speaks Spanish."

"Um, okay... He's Yayi and RJ's dad, though."

"I haven't met yo daddy, but he looks even darker in all those pictures. I didn't know."

"My daddy is Colombian." Giggles left my mouth, but she did not return them.

"He's a Black Colombian," she said.

Tominique's words were snowballs destined to become an avalanche in my adulthood: "a Black man that speaks Spanish." Blackness was a nonexistent topic to Papi. He never brought it up.

* * *

When I was a teen, Papi owned a barbershop. He didn't know the first thing about cutting hair, but God had blessed him with an entrepreneurial mindset from an early age. The shop showcased his name on the outside in illuminated letters, but on the inside, six barbers executed the cuts, braids, and line-ups. At the beginning of each month, they paid Papi a fixed fee—otherwise known as "chair rent"—in order to operate in his shop.

While the barbers worked and he made passive income, Papi floated around like the most popular guy in school. He'd hop in and out of conversations between barbers and patrons, set up the best music playlists, and visit surrounding businesses in the plaza. Everyone from the owners of the pizza parlor to the bakery and market knew Antonio Apolinario.

Out of all the businesses, though, he spent the most time at the beauty salon next door. Papi had gotten to know the owner so well that she offered her services to Windaly and me free of charge. From that day on, I became accustomed to biweekly eyebrow-waxing appointments and three or four hair trims a year. Following each appointment, I lounged around Papi's shop until he took me home. Some days, the wait wasn't long. Other days, long hours passed before I returned to Mami's house.

One day, thirty minutes before closing, I was hanging around the shop when a young Black man stumbled in and scanned the area. He seemed to be in his late teens, either in his final year of high school or a college freshman, and he was sporting a white V-neck T-shirt with black basketball shorts and some Jordans. A cloud of urgency surrounded him.

He locked eyes with Papi, who was in mid-conversation with one of the barbers. I'm not sure how he concluded that Papi owned the shop, but in a split second, the man approached Papi.

"Hey, man. I know the shop is about to close, but I just need a quick line-up, that's all. Y'all take walk-ins?"

Papi gestured across the room. "Yeah. He should be finished in ten minutes, then you can go next."

After Papi spoke, the young man squinted and tilted his head in confusion. But after Papi repeated what he'd said, the puzzled look washed away and was replaced with relief. The young man smiled and exhaled. "Whew, thank you, man! I appreciate it!"

Before the man joined me in the waiting area, a shadow of the perplexed look returned. He opened his mouth with caution. "Hey, where are you from?"

Papi chuckled and raised his chin toward the medium-sized flag in the waiting area. "I'm Colombian, born and raised."

"Wow, man. I thought you were Black! Your accent confused me. I thought you were Jamaican or something."

Papi shook his head. "No sir, I am Colombian, not Black."

For Afro-Latinos like my father, nationalism eclipses race. They love their home country, and they have pride in their nation. Therefore, they identify with their country more than their race. Papi identifies with Colombia before his African roots. The man's inquiry didn't offend him, but that isn't always the case.

Time after time, I've witnessed Afro-Latinos become offended when asked if they're Black, their necks retracting in disbelief.

"No, I'm not Black. I'm Cuban."

"No, I'm not Black. I'm Dominican."

Not too long ago, I came across an alarming video on social media of a Dominican man screaming "I am not Black!" into the camera. The title of the video was "Dominicans are not Black." Brown freckles were sprinkled on the Dominican's honey-coated skin, meeting his ginger-toned hair. 4B curls spiraled from his head to form a two-inch Afro. His eyes were a blend of green and gray hues. The bridge of his nose lay wide across his face and led to large, full lips.

He bore the obvious features of a Black or biracial man. Despite that, he yelled, "Dominicans are not Black! Why do we believe we are Black? We are not Black!" An exasperated pink flush crept over his skin, and a vein protruded from his neck. He yelled the phrases many times as his angry spirit seeped through my phone screen. For reasons unbeknownst to me, calling Dominicans Black struck a nerve for him.

Not all Afro-Latinos share this mindset. For as long as I can remember, my cousin Dayana, Roberto's niece, was always proud of her Afro-Cuban heritage. She handled microaggressions from non-Black people and the Latino community with ease. The harsh truth was that most of her encounters with racism were at the hands of the Latino community.

It was typical to hear people who were unaware of her Cuban ethnicity talk about her in Spanish, similar to Mita meeting Papi back in the day. She's always been naturally self-assured and unaffected. She also has one of the quickest mouths I've ever heard. Whenever these situations arose, she'd snap at her aggressors with the finest obscenities and vulgarity the Cuban culture offers. Then she'd laugh at their stupidity. She is a proud Black Latina. Today, her Instagram bio reads "Cocoa-dipped Cubana and *Cubanita de Chocolatè*."

Afro-Cuban musical artist Celia Cruz was also well-known for showcasing love for her African heritage, which was uncommon in her time. She often belted out the word *azucar*, sugar, in her songs, alluding to the African slaves that worked on Cuba's sugar plantations. She transformed something traumatic into a symbol of power. Many of her songs shed light on her beautiful features, from her lips to the rhythm in her hips.

If someone asked Papi today if he was Black, he would probably reply, "Yes, and Colombian." He no longer laughs at the question. He doesn't look at inquiring African Americans in disbelief. Something changed, and I believe the birth of Papi's Black discovery caused that change. But what is a Black discovery? Even if you choose to ignore the color of your skin, you know you're Black, so how can that be discovered?

Black discovery entails a lot of different things. It's learning unconditional self-love for your Blackness. It's unlearning everything society taught you to hate about yourself. It's reclaiming the African heritage that colonized countries tried to obliterate. It's realizing your Black is beautiful, from your lips to your skin to your hair. It's knowing that every nuance of African DNA is beautiful, regardless of past experiences. It's learning to navigate uncomfortable questions like the infamous "Can I touch your hair?" It's the swell of Black pride in your veins when you learn more about your people—stories of innovation, strength, and courage, instead of the typical slavery narrative.

Journeys of Black discovery vary. For me, Tominique's words on the night I introduced her to my family planted a bug in my ear. I didn't know what the bug was right away, but it buzzed each time I encountered similar discussions until the buzz grew clearer and clearer: I was biracial. I was Black.

Black discovery isn't as dramatic as finding out you're Black. It could be the moment when a Black woman has *the* hair epiphany, the "you don't need a relaxer to be presentable to society" one. It could be learning to love the God-given hair that sprouts from your head. It could be mustering up the confidence to walk into a job interview with Bantu knots, a braided hairstyle, or a big Afro. It's the confidence of a Black man dressed in professional business attire with dreadlocks swaying down his back, a style deemed unkempt by European beauty standards.

For some people, the discovery is self-reflection, a deep conversation with oneself regarding their relationship to the Black community. During this, some questions may arise: Do I uplift my people? Do I circulate wealth back into my community? How many Black businesses do I support? Tougher, more analytical queries may come up: Do I date outside of my race on purpose? If I marry a woman of a different race, will I still show my Black sisters love and respect? Can I talk to my non-Black spouse about the Black experience, or do I need to tone it down? This self-evaluation, a deep cleaning, is vital.

My brother-in-law Terik, also experienced a Black discovery. As a licensed social worker, he often felt the need to cut his hair to a short fade and his facial hair even shorter. He wanted to come off as nonthreatening as possible to his non-Black clients and co-workers.

During one of my holiday visits back home, I greeted him, "Okay, I see you with the clean shave! Looking good!" I laughed and embraced him. It had been quite a while since we'd seen each other.

He let out a hearty laugh as he stroked his chin with his fingers. "Thank you, thank you! Had to shave it, don't wanna scare the White folk!"

A vision of Terik rushed through my mind. I pictured him at work, a counselor at a Florida middle school where one could count all the staff of color on one hand. As he continued to chuckle, my smile dissipated. He made light of the situation, but it was crazy that something as minuscule as a beard could label him as more threatening.

Months later, there was a shift. Now, Terik lets his beard grow as long as he wants. He sports an Afro or cornrows and never passes up an opportunity to show love for his Black brothers and sisters. He no longer feels the need to adjust his appearance. His expertise and amazing personality carry him in the workplace, not a short fade or a lack of facial hair.

My father is a man of few words, so it's hard to pinpoint the details of his Black discovery. He didn't grow an Afro or a beard like Terik; a tidal wave of Black pride didn't inflate his chest. Yet, something shifted. He started talking more about Afro-Colombian culture, things I wouldn't have known otherwise.

He spoke of influential Afro-Colombian musical artists, such as Joe Arroyo and Grupo Niche, and introduced me to Champeta, an Afro-Colombian style of dance. He delved into his memories of life in Chocó and taught me about San Basilio de Palenque or, as the locals call it, Palenque, a Black town where escaped slaves would find refuge. I was shocked to learn that Palenque is still around today and that its African culture was preserved in such a unique way. The locals even speak a Creole language, a mixture between Spanish and Kikongo, an African language spoken in Congo and Angola. Papi even shared his dislike for the nickname "Negro" many non-Black Latinos give him, regardless of whether it's a term of endearment or not.

The entire air around his Blackness and his identity shifted, and now it's no longer an unspoken or overlooked topic. His Black discovery occurred late in his life, but again, the timeline and experiences differ from person to person. Perhaps my discovery sparked his. He listened to the topics I began discussing in my early adulthood. He read my pro-Black social media posts and even liked a few. He also noticed when I started referring to myself as an Afro-Latina. Seeing me go through my journey may have sparked his.

My Black discovery was a journey of learning—learning that I was Black, and learning about the African Diaspora in Latin America and the heavy influences we had on the culture. I revisited comments I had heard as a child with clear ears, giving them their true name: microaggressions.

I learned to love the physical characteristics my Black side was responsible for, those that outside people made me feel inferior about.

In addition to learning to love myself, I learned to love all my Black brothers and sisters around me, the whole Diaspora, no matter where they came from.

CHAPTER 8

Shade Twin

His jawline was defined and sharp. A rich, dark-chocolate hue took up every inch of his skin. Everything from his color to his features mirrored Papi to perfection. In awe, I studied his every move, every mannerism. I couldn't believe it! I had finally met my brother Deivy Apolinario.

When I was a child, Papi showed me pictures of my brother in Colombia from a previous marriage. But now he was moving to the States where we would finally get to meet one another. However, no number of pictures could prepare me for what I saw. Not only did I find Papi in Deivy's face, but I also saw my own. We looked alike. I was staring at a manly, melanin-filled version of me! It baffled my fifteen-year-old brain.

There's no denying that Windaly and I resemble Papi, but something about Deivy's face tied it all together. Windaly's face always took after Papi's while mine teetered between Mami's and Papi's, landing in a mostly indistinguishable place between. Some people couldn't tell who I resembled. But somehow, Deivy and I favored each other, and it blew my mind to smithereens. I, too, had a shade twin.

Anthony Apolinario, my eldest brother, favors Papi. Still, his beautiful mother, Nohemy, may she rest in peace, shines through in his facial features as well. Because he's a delicate mix of the two, Anthony resembled whichever parent he was standing next to at the moment. His skin is a silky mocha tone, a little lighter than Deivy and Papi's.

Since Anthony was raised in Colombia but born in the United States, moving back to the US was an easier process for him. However, Deivy was born in Colombia and couldn't move to the States until about 2010, after completing all the steps required by US Immigration. I met my first long-lost brother from Colombia, Anthony, when I was ten. Now, I stood before my second brother. Here he was in the flesh, outside of a still photograph.

Deivy scanned the room, peeping over at Windaly and then at Anthony, met my eyes, and halted his gaze on Papi, seated on the other side of the room. He looked like he was about to decipher a math equation. After shifting his eyes back to Windaly, he asked, "Espera un minuto, cuantos años tienes? Cuando es tu cumpleaños?" *Wait a minute, how old are you? When's your birthday?*

"Veinte años. Nací el veintiséis de Marzo de mil noveceintos noventa y uno." *Twenty. I was born on March 26, 1991.*

Once again, his gaze met mine, and then it returned to Windaly. "Y cuanto años tiene Yorelis?" *And how old is Yorelis?*

"Ella tiene quince años." *She's fifteen years old.*

The confusion dissipated from his face. He once again

glanced at our father across the room. Papi was talking, entirely unaware of his children's conversation. Deivy looked at Windaly, shook his head, and, from the deepest part of his core, let out a hearty chuckle. "Este hombre es demasiado!" *This man is too much!*

His laugh was infectious, and we started chuckling, too.

"Por que preguntaste? Que paso?" *Why'd you ask? What happened?*

"Nací el treinta y uno de Abril, mil novecientos noventa y tres." *I was born on Abril 29, 1993.*

Like the flip of a switch, Windaly's "lightbulb" turned on. Deivy's spontaneous laughter, his comment about Papi, his FBI-level interrogation regarding our birthdays... The dots connected: Deivy was born between Windaly and me, during Papi's relationship with Mami! We exploded into full-on laughter.

We all had different relationships with Papi. His presence in our lives varied and so did our opinions about him. But at that moment, Anthony, Deivy, Windaly, and I could agree on one thing: Papi loved beautiful women. They were his kryptonite. Therefore, he didn't always make the wisest decisions when it came to them.

When I was little, I remember taking trips around Tampa with Papi. He'd pick me up from Mami's house on designated weekends and complete whatever errands needing doing that day. We would stop by a friend's house, a grocery store, or the local Colombian bakery for my favorite bread, pan de bono. As soon as we entered any building, his walk morphed into cool, slow strides. His chest poked forward, and his eyes scanned his surroundings with confidence, playfully bouncing from one woman's backside to another. Even then, I noticed Papi's behavior.

One day, after we had spent the afternoon together, it was time to take me back to Mami's house. He escorted me to the front door, exchanged a few formal words with Mami, and made his way back to the car. I immediately leaped onto the living room sofa and separated the curtains a bit to observe Papi with the most patience a little girl could muster.

Once he had reversed out of our cul-de-sac, I whipped around to Mami, uncontrollable giggles erupting from my gut. "Mami! Mami! I have something funny to say!"

"Que, mi amor?"

"Papi always looks at ladies' butts when we go places!"

A small smile formed in the corner of her lips and then crept over her entire mouth. She raised her eyebrows high in sarcastic surprise. "Oh, really?"

"So as long he's watching you the same way he's watching those butts, we won't have a problem!"

By that point, Mami knew what kind of man her husband was. That behavior was one of many things that led to the demise of their marriage. She hadn't held onto residual feelings, but she was thankful he was another woman's problem. Now, she could finally sit back, relax, and laugh at all his foolish games.

* * *

Following the grand discovery about our brother, Windaly and I told Mami.

Clutching her stomach, Mami threw her head back and

released high-volume laughter. "Nena, that was probably one of your father's business trips to Colombia!"

The news left her unfazed. Anyone that knew Antonio Apolinario was also unfazed.

After his relationships with Nohemy and Mami, Papi found himself with someone else: a gorgeous, olive-toned woman named Luz Marie. Her thick, dark-brown, never-ending hair laid flat on her back. But with each step, it swayed from left to right across her hips. Her eyes were small and slanted, and every time she flashed her high-cheekbone smile, her eyes thinned out even more.

I often wondered if Luz Marie was Asian and Colombian; there must be a reason this woman had such tight eyes.

Now, I'm more familiar with the different flavors that makeup of South American genealogy.

In addition to Indigenous inhabitants and Spanish colonizers, there were later mass migrations from Asian countries to South America. Today, I wouldn't be surprised if Luz Marie's DNA results revealed Indigenous, Spanish, and Asian contributions. Like many folks, her genetic makeup may reflect a dense melting pot of cultures.

With the combination of Papi's small, almond-shaped eyes and Luz Marie's even smaller, regal eyes, their son—my little brother Xavier Apolinario—came into this world with the tiniest and most expressive eyes. Xavier is Papi's youngest child, falling between Yayi's and RJ's ages. Xavier's mixed-race genes produced a caramel-chocolate skin tone, almost identical to Anthony's mocha. Since he was an infant, full 4B/4C curls have corkscrewed from his scalp. Surprisingly, he grew taller than all his siblings and parents; no telling where he inherited that gene from.

It was routine for me to live with Mami and Roberto and then go to Papi's house on the weekends. We never used labels like half brother or half sister—they were just my siblings. Despite meeting Anthony and Deivy later, I grew comfortable having them in my life. My family structure was far from "normal," but it was mine.

Discovering that Deivy was conceived between Windaly and me was a curveball, but I didn't have strong opinions about it. I was content. I had met my brothers, my blood, and they now lived down the street.

I was blessed with an opportunity to strengthen my relationship with my Colombian side. My family was complete —or at least, I believed it was.

CHAPTER 9

Another Business Trip

A ntonio entered the party with a determined, wide-legged waddle, three-year-old Windaly trailing behind him. Windy fell third in line to keep an eye on her growing toddler. Warmth filled her heart as she took in her surroundings, digesting every detail.

This was it—her new life in Colombia alongside her husband and their baby girl! The small town of Juana Díaz where everyone knew La Hija de Kikin, Kikin's daughter, was in the past. Here, no one outside of her husband's family knew her, and her life was free from the microscope of the Juana Díaz bochinche, *gossip*. She no longer had to navigate Spanish and broken English like she did in Tampa as, once again, her native language flooded her ears. Cali was a fresh start.

Friends and family were scattered throughout the home, and the atmosphere was boisterous and high-spirited. The smell of seasoned Colombian food filled her nostrils while rhythmic salsa music and vibrant conversation played in her ears. People who were eager to meet Antonio's daughter made their way to Windaly in clusters.

"Ay Dios mío, ella es hermosa Windy!" *She's beautiful, Windy!*

"Mira Antonio, ella se parece a ti!" *Look Antonio, she looks like you!*

"Mira el hermoso cabello rizado!" *Look at her gorgeous curly hair!*

Everyone was floored by the new addition to the family.

Joy overwhelmed every part of Windy's being. As the festivities went on, she spoke with family members, laughed, danced, and chased Windaly everywhere her little legs took her.

A few shots of aguardiente later, some partygoers were celebrating a little more loosely. People sang along to songs as if they were Joe Arroyo, and a few men shouted stories and jokes over the music. People filled their hungry stomachs with a vengeance.

Windy relaxed on the sofa with Windaly fighting sleep on her lap. The toddler laid against Windy's chest with her feet dangling and eyes rolling to the back of her head, but she was refusing to succumb to the slumber. This battle was standard in Windy's household; no matter what fight her three-year-old put up, sleep would dominate eventually.

While rocking the toddler to sleep, Windy glanced at her husband across the room. Antonio was sitting with a few cousins in a circle of chairs. They were laughing, drinking, and reminiscing about their younger days.

One of them took a swig from his drink and locked eyes with Windy. He paused, smiled from ear to ear, and then turned back to his cousin. He said in Spanish, "Antonio, let me tell you something. Your daughter is so gorgeous! So beautiful! And it's crazy; she looks like you, unlike the other girl."

Windy's chest stiffened. Tending to Windaly, rocking her and wiping faint traces of drool from her mouth, Windy pretended she hadn't heard the man. But her mind was flipping through an obstacle course of thoughts: The other little girl? What little girl? My husband has one other child, and that's Anthony. Why did his cousin look at her and say that? Is he trying to create drama?

Though Windy's mind was spiraling, she remained quiet until later that night. When she confronted her husband, he said she had misunderstood everything. Windy was overrun with emotions and exhausted from the party, so she decided to bury it in her subconscious.

Years later, when they returned to Tampa, this memory from Colombia stayed. And once they had finalized their divorce in 1996, the memory was so suppressed that she had almost forgotten about it.

Tampa, Florida, 2014

"Yoyi!" Mami called from the living room.

"Qué es?" I hollered from my bedroom.

"Ven aca! Tengo algo que enseñarte!" *Come here! I have something to show you!*

My mother always had an uncanny ability to call me when I was most comfortable. This time, I was in bed, the fuzzy comforter swallowing me to perfection. Nonetheless, I put my house slippers on and made my way to the living room. In the sala, Mami was lounging on the sofa, also cocooned in a blanket, with her eyes glued to her phone.

"What did you wanna show me, Mami?"

"Ven sientate. Mira esta foto de tu hermana." *Come sit. Look at this picture of your sister.*

What? A picture of my sister? She called me here for a picture?! In my mind, I performed the largest eye roll possible. Of course, if I had ever mustered up enough courage to actually do that in front of my mother, I wouldn't have eyes to repeat the offense with.

"Mami, you called me over here to look at a picture of Windaly or Yayi?"

She smiled. "No, mija. This is your other sister."

She flipped her phone screen toward me. A pretty, mocha-colored Black woman stared back. Her small eyes slanted above her high, defined cheekbones.

"Really? Who is this? Did Roberto have another daughter in Cuba?"

Mami shook her head and giggled.

"What? No, mija. This is your father's other daughter, Mayara."

She had traces of Papi's features. In fact, she favored Xavier, Papi's youngest. A faint ringing formed in my ears. What did she just tell me? Was this some random bochinche, *gossip?*

Long story short, Papi had another daughter, Mayara, nicknamed Maya. Like Deivy, she was also born between Windaly and me—a likely outcome of another one of my father's "business trips" to Colombia. Mami told me about Papi's cousin "accidentally" letting the secret slip some years ago when Maya was about one year old. And there I was at eighteen, three years after meeting Deivy and eight years after meeting Anthony. I thought I had met all my long-lost siblings. Then again, I know the type of man my father is.

A few months later, Papi sent me a picture of Maya through WhatsApp and wrote, "This is your sister, my other daughter Maya." No further details, no explanation—just those words.

Shifting my focus onto my newest sister and away from Papi's antics, I replied, "Wow, she is gorgeous!"

Maya searched for us on Facebook. She found my mother first and sent her a friend request. I virtually connected with her months before my father revealed the "big secret" to his children. If Maya had never taken the initiative, would Papi have ever told us?

I am more than grateful for all the blood relatives God has blessed me with. However, I sometimes wish my father hadn't lived his life free of any thoughts about consequences, ones that would inevitably fall onto his children.

I could've built a relationship with Mayara years ago. Regardless, she is here now. I decided to focus on strengthening my relationship with her instead of resenting my father.

CHAPTER 10

I didn't know I was Black

I have always noticed the various skin tones in my family tree. My Afro-Colombian/Afro-Cuban family embodied all shades, from light-skinned to mocha to dark chocolate, and they all held influential positions in my life. I practiced an Afro-Cuban religion from West Africa, Santería or Lucumí, for most of my life. I wasn't aware of its African origins, but I knew that non-Black Latinos referred to the faith as "La regla de los Negros," *the religion of the Black people.*

I was a kid with mixed-race features, but somehow I didn't know I was Black. It's difficult to wrap my head around how this could be true, but I really didn't know.

Growing up Afro-Latinidad, Blackness wasn't a hot topic in my household. I'd heard my father tell another young Black man that he was not Black. He tethered his identity to his home country, not his race. Back then, I'd never heard people say, "I'm Afro-Colombian."

Afro-Latinidad was only to be addressed when talking about musical artists or African deities in Roberto's religion.

Absorbing what I saw around me, I learned to cling to my nationality, too, thus forming a thick color-blind lens.

Whenever Papi and Roberto stood before me, I saw a Cuban man and a Colombian man, never two men of African descent—never two Black men. When someone asked about my race, I told them I was just Puerto Rican and Colombian. That lens misconstrued my racial identity so much that I confused the people around me.

* * *

My dance classes and competitions were hardly at the top of Papi's list of priorities. Still, he made a few appearances. When I was thirteen, he attended his first competition and sat through all the routines. Dance competitions can last from sunrise to sundown, so Papi proved to be quite the trooper. Our dances received high adjudications; the hard work and long practices seemed to have paid off.

Following the awards ceremony, our dance troupe left the stage and walked cheerfully to the lobby. One of the first faces I recognized in the crowd was Papi's. I quickened my steps, opened my arms, and gave my father the most enormous hug my tiny frame could offer. As our arms unraveled, I turned to some of my friends in the dance company and announced, "Guys, this is my dad!"

The girls smiled, said hello, and then excused themselves to go find their families. I had no words back then to describe the feeling in the air, but it was tense and thick.

We returned to dance class the following Monday to continue our training and prepare for the next competition. After grueling across-the floor-combinations, our ballet teacher, released us for a water break. I was waiting my turn at the water fountain when one of my classmates tapped my shoulder.

"Hey!"

"Hey!" I spun around. "What's up?"

"Your dad is Black? I never knew! Why didn't you tell us?"

I gave her a puzzled look. "What? My dad isn't Black. He's Colombian."

"Huh?"

"He's Colombian," I repeated. "He speaks Spanish."

Her confused expression now matched mine.

"Oh...well, okay." She shrugged her shoulders and giggled, and we left it at that.

But an uneasy feeling trickled into my body. The exchange felt odd: her smirk, something about the way "Black" rolled off her tongue, as if it was a rumor in elementary school or the name of a secret crush. She surrounded the question with a taunting, analytical air, yet the moment had passed so quickly. I drank from the fountain and then returned to dance class.

A few months later, a young man waltzed into Papi's barbershop and asked him the same question. Why did Papi's race mystify so many? In reality, others weren't confused; I was. As the years went by, similar experiences happened here and there. Every year, I'm reminded by Facebook Memories of a status posted by the racially confused, fifteen-year-old Yorelis in April 2010: "He asked me if I was Black? Lol! Do I look Black?!" The status refers to an experience at a local mall in Tampa with my cousin Dayanara.

Like most teenagers, Dayanara and I spent countless

hours at the mall doing absolutely nothing. We walked enough circles to win a five-mile race and window-shopped enough to build an essay-length Christmas wish list. We studied all the teen eye candy and even exchanged Myspace profiles with a few. Every other weekend, the mall was our official hangout.

One weekend, while Dayanara and I were strolling through the mall, a group of teenage boys with flirty energy stopped us. They asked us what school we went to, how old we were, and if we had boyfriends. When they asked if we could become Myspace friends, my cousin and I declined. They were polite, but they weren't our type (though I'm not even sure what type my teenage self preferred).

We had brought the conversation to a close and were walking away when one boy called after me, "Hey, wait! Can I ask you something else real quick?"

I paused, taking a baby step back. "Yeah, what's up?"

He stepped closer. "Are you Black? Like, are you mixed?"

"Ha! No, I'm Puerto Rican and Colombian, not Black."

"Oh, damn! I thought you were mixed. I thought you was, like, a Tia and Tamera type." He tilted his head.

"Oh, naw! I'm just Hispanic, but thank you, though! They're beautiful. Have a good day!"

I walked away, utterly confused. How was the same situation that happened with Papi happening to me? And that's when I signed in to my new Facebook account and posted my status: "He asked me if I was Black? Lol! Do I look Black?!"

My idea of my racial identity was discombobulated, but out of all the family members and dance moms that followed me on Facebook, no one corrected me. There have been multiple instances where I've said, "No, I'm not Black." And each time, the adults who knew my family never corrected me. I continued on with my warped racial identity. With a father as chocolate as Wesley Snipes, it's difficult to fathom how I denied half of my racial identity for so long, but I did.

CHAPTER 11

Complicated Relationships

Despite the confusing experiences, by sixteen, I had somehow realized I was half Black.

I knew that Papi was a Black man from Colombia. The reason why Black people were there to begin with remained a mystery to me, but I still had many moons to go in my Black discovery.

I didn't know about African slavery outside of the United States until I was around eighteen, but at sixteen, I knew I was biracial. That much I could make sense of. I was still uncertain, though, about the way I would identify myself to the outside world. When asked the infamous question about "what I was," I answered differently every time.

"I'm just Puerto Rican."

"I'm Puerto Rican and Colombian."

"I'm mixed."

"I'm Puerto Rican and Black."

"I'm Black and White."

. . .

"I'm just Puerto Rican" and "I'm Puerto Rican and Black" stemmed from my complicated relationship with Papi back then. In addition to his inconsistent presence in my life, there was a domestic violence incident with my stepmother, Luz Marie, whom I adored with every bone in my body.

With the mixture of Mami's famous Renovales teachings and my maturing feminist mindset, I saw red when I heard what Papi had done to my stepmother. I'd be damned if any man related to me, by blood or not, put his hands on a woman.

Around this time, Papi also moved to Costa Rica because of an arrest warrant for unpaid child support. These situations caused a rift in our relationship, which didn't smooth over until recently. Back then, things were rough. I wanted nothing to do with Papi—in other words, "to hell with my daddy."

So when someone asked what I was, I told them I was just Puerto Rican. If they were asking because of my complexion or hair, I would say I was Puerto Rican and Black to ease their confusion. But this also erased Papi from the equation. Sixteen-year-old Yorelis wanted nothing more than to sever the connection to her Colombian side and everything else related to her father.

Spanish and I have always been in a complicated relationship. It was never toxic, but we had our fair share of ups and downs. I'm not fluent now.

But if you ask my mother, Spanish was the only language I spoke until I entered pre-K, where I was ridiculed for not speaking English. According to Mami, that's when the shift began. I stopped speaking Spanish altogether. As I learned more in school, English became the only language to escape my mouth. I'm not insinuating that Mami is a liar, but I don't recall ever being able to speak Spanish or being ridiculed for it. Perhaps I was just too young.

If you ask me, the cause of my complicated relationship with Spanish is that I did not grow up speaking the language. As a child, every adult addressed me in Spanish, but I replied in English. No one instructed me otherwise.

Putting myself in the shoes of a primarily Spanish-speaking adult, it's easy to live in Town 'n' Country, Tampa, without speaking English.

TC is filled with Latinos. The chances of having Spanish-speaking doctors, customers, and co-workers are very high. Mita has lived in Tampa for more than thirty years and still hasn't learned to speak English well! She has only run into a few situations where she needed to speak English.

If someone doesn't speak English, they might practice with their child, niece, nephew, or cousin. Adults tend to be more comfortable practicing English with kids; children unknowingly provide a safe place for the adults to work through their accents and perhaps even crash and burn. I recall multiple instances where Mita or Papi repeated English words, using our conversations to get some practice in.

Whether it's because of school bullies or never being required to speak the language, I'm not a fluent Spanish speaker. My comprehension includes profanity, informal conversation, some easy reading, and Caribbean dialects (Puerto Rican, Cuban, and Dominican). Plop me in front of a formal Spanish documentary, and I'll be as useless as a broken hair tie.

People in my life have had varying opinions on my broken Spanish, and most have never thought twice about sharing them with me.

"Suenas como una gringa!" *You sound like a white girl!*

"No eres realmente Puertorriqueña." *You aren't really Puerto Rican.*

"Como tienes dos padres que hablan español y no hablas español?" *How do you have two Spanish-speaking parents and you don't speak Spanish?*

The list goes on.

Often, if someone doesn't remark on my broken Spanish, a tone of disappointment creeps in with the realization. My most recent experience with this occurred during a phone call with my aunt Tia Tocalla, Papi's blood sister in Colombia.

Papi didn't reconnect with his birth family until later in his life. Because of this, I met Tocalla and my grandmother Carlina when I was twenty-three. The meeting was virtual through WhatsApp. In the beginning, I spoke to them with Papi at my side. He dictated most of the conversations, and I chimed in for the small talk.

Lately, they've been reaching out via video call when I'm not with Papi. I survived the first two calls, each lasting about twenty minutes. But by the end of the third call, the cat was out of the bag.

After a few incorrect verb conjugations and a lot of "Qué dijiste?"—*What did you say?*—Tia Tocalla paused, staring into the camera.

"No hablas español?" she asked.

"No mi español no es muy bueno, pero quiero practicar

más." *No, my Spanish isn't perfect, but I want to practice more.*

My shoulders slumped. I thought I could've continued a while longer before being exposed, but God had other plans. Nowadays, I'm a little more patient. With more practice and less timidity, I'll improve my ability to speak fluently. However, from the age of sixteen to nineteen, that was not the case for me.

Like most teenagers, emotion dictated a great deal of my actions, and I had a plethora of emotions. I was fed up with people deeming me "not Puerto Rican." My eye twitched each time someone said I sounded like a *gringa*. I felt disconnected from my community.

So, during my teens, when asked about my ethnicity, I said I was White American and Black American. That's it. That answer often stopped people in their tracks.

The days of Latinos releasing Spanish onto my ears were long gone. Critiques and opinions ceased to reach me. This newfound identity calmed my anxiety about speaking Spanish, and it was accurate. Racially mother is White, and my father is Black. Before hearing the twang of their accents or noticing their Spanish names, no one suspected anything else. Although this answer suited my anxiety at the time, I didn't fool any Caribbean Latino over the age of eighteen. My name practically screamed Puerto Rican.

After moving to Los Angeles and being exposed to an assortment of cultures, I noticed distinguishing traits for each ethnic group. For example, it's common for Armenians to bear a last name that ends in "-ian" or "-yan." So when the Kardashian family reached stardom, Armenians understood they were looking at one of their own.

The same phenomenon applies to Puerto Rican and some other Caribbean cultures. For some reason, Puerto Ricans love the sound of "-lis" (pronounced *lease*) at the end of a girl's name, like Yorelis (*yo-reh-lease*).

If we scanned my Puerto Rican family tree, we'd find my cousins named

Maricelis (*ma-ree-seh-lease*)

Amariliz (*am-ah-ree-lease*), and

Mireliz (*me-reh-lease*)

In middle school, I had a classmate named Arelys (*ah-reh-lease*), who was also Puerto Rican. I've encountered many Cuban and Dominican women with the same sort of name as well.

My last name caused some of my failed attempts to identify as Black and White. With Greek and Filipino origins, the name "Apolinario" is still uncommon in Latin culture. It is common in the Philippines, Brazil, and Ecuador, but that's about it. Therefore, Apolinario isn't as revealing of my heritage. But "Yorelis" shrieks Caribbean. There's no way to hide it.

By the time I was nineteen, the need to separate from my Latinidad diminished. I became more patient with my complex relationship with Spanish, took baby steps, and refused to allow embarrassment to take over when my words were muddled.

Today, I maintain the same steps. I try to implement more Caribbean-dialect Spanish, but that can be difficult when living in a Central-American community in Los Angeles.

My focus has also shifted to understanding the Colombian dialect. My relationships with my aunt and grandmother continue to grow, and my dream is to visit Colombia for the first time and meet them in person. And when that moment finally arrives, I want to spend less time asking, "Qué dijiste?"

CHAPTER 12

Black and Colombian, or Afro-Colombian?

TAMPA, FLORIDA, 2015

I was nineteen, preparing for one of the most monumental steps in my life—moving to Los Angeles, California. The roller-coaster ride around my racial identity was reaching a plateau. When someone asked what I was, I answered, "I'm Puerto Rican and Colombian." If the person continued to act perplexed, I followed up with more detail: "I'm Puerto Rican and Colombian, but my daddy is Black and Colombian." Almost every time, those who lingered on the question were Black people.

Most Black people have a keen radar when it comes to identifying one of their own. If a person's features don't give it away, sometimes we can still sense it. Years ago, when we first met, Sheopatra asked the infamous question, "What are you?"

I responded in the normal way. "I'm Puerto Rican and Colombian."

"Okay, but who's Black?" she asked a half second later.

It caught me by surprise. Who's Black? How did she know? Most people were still unaware that Latinos could also be Black. (Those same people probably loved Zoe Saldaña or Don Omar. Go figure.)

I clarified, "My dad is Afro-Colombian. He's Black but was born and raised in Colombia." She understood immediately.

The more I connected with my Black side, the more I developed my own radar. When I met my LA friend Blair, something about her felt Black. Despite her strong Asian features and thick, straight hair, Black vibrations emanated from her spirit. Her skin was a silky, mocha-caramel color, but that didn't necessarily indicate Black American. She could have been of Filipino heritage; there are plenty dark-skinned Filipinos. There are a lot of dark Asians in general.

Still, in my heart of hearts, I knew Blair gave off another flavor—the flavor of a Black girl. She didn't speak a particular way; overflowing Ebonics didn't fill her vocabulary. She also didn't meet the other stereotypical Black traits deemed by society. But she had a little something.

Come to find out, Blair's mother is Black and her father, Korean. My wife told me she had a similar experience when they met years ago. Something in her also perceived Blair as a Black woman. That nagging sense, that radar, provided the hunch. Having used that inner radar personally, I recognize when it's directed at me. I can sense the persistent question in the air, despite my given answer. Back then, if I used the term Afro-Latino instead of Black and Colombian, people got more confused.

The year 2015 was not a long time ago. The term "Afro-Latino" existed, but it hadn't made its way to the mainstream. There have been multiple instances where I was met with befuddled, almost offended reactions after using the term.

White people often comment, "What is that? How exotic!"

Latinos, often non-Black, resort to "What's with all the labeling? That creates unwelcome division in our community. Why does your generation do that?"

Black people, those uneducated on Africans outside of the US, are either surprised or insulted. "Is that even real? Wow, Hispanics love to make stuff up to be Black." Or they'd say, "Whoa, I had no idea Afro-Latinos existed."

I've heard almost every rebuttal under the sun.

I'd always try my best to explain, beginning with how the Portuguese and Spanish also participated in the transatlantic slave trade. I would travel through history and end by telling them how Africans and their descendants remain in these colonized regions today. In the past, one of the toughest concepts for Black Americans to grasp was that all-Black Afro-Latinos exist. By "all Black," I mean 100 percent Black, without mixed-race features. I mean those like Antonio Apolinario and Roberto Gutierrez: chocolate-colored, melanin-filled people with Black features who are not mixed.

When it comes to Afro-Latinos, people can get tunnel vision around a certain look. It teeters around loose, curly hair, light-chocolate skin, and other mixed-race features. It's rare for dark Godiva chocolates to come to mind when discussing Afro-Latinos, despite how many of them mirror that complexion. Even when I tell someone that my father is Afro-Latino or Afro-Colombian, more often than not, that person is still surprised when they see a picture of Papi.

"Wow! I didn't know he was *Black* Black."

"Dang, yo daddy dark!"

For whatever reason, they had probably envisioned a light-skinned or mixed-race Black man. Maybe they were expecting a picture of Chris Brown or Drake.

CHAPTER 13

SHE

There had to have been at least six hundred people ready to audition. I lined up at about seven in the morning and left around eight that night. Though I waited around for most of the day, the bulk of my audition took twenty minutes. Gotta love cattle calls, right?

A cattle call is an audition that has hundreds of attendees. Because of the many candidates, the audition often lasts all day, and most of it is filled with gruesome waiting. I met Sheopatra, or She, at this cattle call.

Her artist name, SHEstreet, stems from her ode to female empowerment, SHE, and her mother's maiden name, Streeter. The dance styles she thrives in are popping, Memphis Jookin', and house, which are all considered street styles of dance and also contributed to her name.

"Yorelis? That's beautiful! Do you have a nickname?" she asked.

"My family calls me Yoyi."

We hit it off right away, laughing and joking as if we already knew one another. Because of her, most of that treacherous waiting at the audition wasn't so bad. We exchanged numbers afterward.

She texted me later that night, "Hey, Yoe! It was so nice to meet you!"

Hm, I thought. I've never seen my name spelled like that before. It was cute, almost like an American version of Yoyi. I've been spelling my name "Yoe" ever since.

At that time, I still hadn't moved to LA. I was visiting during my college spring break. My moving date wasn't until four months later, but I was grateful to have met She. Knowing at least one more person in LA calmed my nerves. On that short list of acquaintances, She was one more person I could connect to and dance with.

A month before the move, she reached out to me with some news. She was starting an all-girl dance company or, in her words, "a collective of queens." The group was called The Council.

She wanted to create a safe space in the dance industry where women could connect and feel supported—a place where powerful female dancers could combine instead of being pitted against one another.

Sheopatra asked if I was interested in being a member once I moved. My insides were a mushy medley of honor, disbelief, excitement, and intimidation. After swiftly stalking her Instagram, and after having witnessed her at the audition, I realized Sheo was one of the most talented dancers I had ever met. That opinion holds true to my heart today.

In this male-dominated industry, the power and strength she carries outweigh a lot of the men's. She moves freely and effortlessly. The source from which she pulls her gifts cannot be identified or replicated. Although I'd only known her for a short time, she quickly became one of my biggest inspirations. So, when she asked me to be a member of The Council, anxiety filled my body.

I'd spent the greater half of my dance education training in classical styles, such as ballet, jazz, and contemporary. I had just begun my street style–based training earlier that year. How did she believe I was worthy enough to be a member of her group? Whatever the reason, she saw it light-years before I did.

Within a few months, I officially moved to LA, became a member of The Council, and called Sheopatra one of my closest friends. Whether we were training, doing video shoots, or just hanging out, I spent most of my free time at her house. During those hanging sessions, I discovered the side of Sheo that would forever broaden my mind.

Instead of the typical scary movie, reality-TV show, or Tyler Perry movie most of my friends watched, she put on *Let the Fire Burn, The Black Power Mixtape, Resurrecting Black Wall Street*, and anything else regarding Black history. When we weren't watching Black-history films, we listened to greats such as Anita Baker and Marvin Gaye, Black artists who were unfamiliar to me and my Latino upbringing.

Sheopatra expressed her beliefs—a lot. She'd pour her heart out about poverty in Black and Brown neighborhoods, and before you knew it, she'd backtrack to redlining, segregation, and slavery. I learned so much from Sheopatra. Each and every time I hung out with her, I knew I was in for the mental ride of my life.

The education I was given at her house blew me away. Despite completing a K–12 education and a year and a half in college, I still had no knowledge of the history she was teaching me. Black history is American history; the two are so deeply interwoven, one cannot exist without the other. So why does the public school system, at least the one I graduated from, present White-American history as the end-all, be-all?

Indeed, February is Black History Month, but it's nothing more than a review of the same eight-to-ten influential Black folks in American history: MLK, Harriet Tubman, Rosa Parks.

Where are the in-depth lessons on Angela Davis and James Baldwin?

Why didn't I learn that Black people invented the traffic light, electric railway, telephone transmitter, and other monumental inventions?

I heard about Muhammad Ali my whole life. America prides itself on the boxing legend and his famous phrase, "Float like a butterfly, sting like a bee." When discussing the greats of boxing, his name is always brought up, but the adversity he faced outside of the ring is pushed aside.

Along with other Black athletes, Muhammad Ali represented the United States in the Olympics, won a gold medal, and then returned home to inhumane treatment and Jim Crow laws. My school made it seem like racial tension was at its peak during the civil rights era. Then Martin Luther King Jr. made a speech that solved everything. Rainbows and gumdrops fell from the sky while everyone joined hands and sang "We Are the World."

I had no idea that Nixon's War on Drugs purposely targeted Black and Brown neighborhoods. I had no clue the KKK still existed, held rallies, and intimidated certain communities. What about when the US government labeled

1970s Black Power groups, who were advocating for equality and better resources, as threats to the American people? I was taught that the Black Panther Party was a militant, nearly terroristic group of radicals.

Through Sheo, I learned they were battling for the many rights Black folks are still fighting for today: community protection, the end of police brutality, and genuine equality for Black Americans.

The Panthers started an effective breakfast program for children in their community, which the public school system adopted years later. Like it did to many other Black civil rights organizations, the US government infiltrated and dismantled the Panthers. Their history was then written by the biased forces remaining in power.

Sheo asked if I knew about the Young Lords, another human rights organization similar to the Black Panthers that was focused on empowering Puerto Ricans and other Latinos. I had no idea what she was talking about. I'd never heard of such a thing. Once again, I was blown away.

As I was learning about America's suppressed Black history, she also introduced me to multiple issues within the Black community, problems established by White Americans and most of which originated during slavery: Uncle Tom syndrome, light skin versus dark skin, and the crabs-in-a-barrel mentality. She touched on *everything*.

As I became more aware of the lasting effects these issues have had on the Black community, the problems hit me harder and harder. They resonated with me even more because the Latino community also suffers from such issues. We have our Uncle Toms. We aspire to reach European standards of beauty instead of accepting the beauty God granted us. Similar to American culture, we have many derogatory terms to describe Black Latinos, yet the word *blanco* stands alone.

If an expecting mother is a White Latino and the father is a Black Latino, friends and family have no restraint announcing their prayer to God: "*Ay Dios Mío*, I hope the baby doesn't come out with the father's hair!"

I always study the Black people in the room when this happens. Sometimes their eyes go blank, and they seem unfazed by or disconnected from what just transpired.

Other times, they agree by describing the "terrible" texture of their own hair. When I heard such statements come from Black people, even as a child, I was infuriated. I wondered, Why do they feel that way? Who told them their hair wasn't pretty? I prize the texture they try so hard to chemically straighten; why don't they?

During my upbringing, people always favored fairer skin over darker skin. On multiple occasions, people—often White Latinos—remarked, "You look just like your dad, but prettier," or, "You look just like your dad but not quemada, *burnt*."

Despite the supposed color blindness in the Latino community, Black Latinos were always the first to be judged or ridiculed. I heard expressions like "Negro sucio," *dirty Black man*, or "Negro peligroso," *dangerous Black man*, more often than any other racial slur. As a matter of fact, phrases about Black Latinos cultivated by White or non-Black Latinos were engraved in my psyche long before I knew that "beaner" and "wetback" were derogatory terms used by White Americans. That in itself speaks volumes.

Once Sheopatra jump-started my Black-history journey, I never looked back.

In my spare time, I watched more documentaries and read books on Black historical figures like Stokely Carmichael and Assata Shakur. The African part of my heritage intrigued me. I wondered what slavery was like in the Caribbean. On that path, I learned that because Willie Lynch successfully "controlled" slaves in the Caribbean, they brought him to America to do the same thing.

By reading *War Against All Puerto Ricans* by Nelson Antonio Denis, I discovered the unlawful experimentation the US government committed on Puerto Ricans in the 1950s and '60s. By this point, I was not blown away. It also did not surprise me to learn that the US government dismantled the Puerto Rican Nationalist Party, which had advocated for decolonization and independence from the US.

Everything I've mentioned is just the tip of the iceberg. So much knowledge was coming at me from various directions. There I was in Los Angeles, outside the bubble that was Town 'n' Country.

My newfound position allowed me to revisit every comment from Mita, my friends, and the rest of my family that I had shrugged away. I could now hear the comments about Afro-Latinos with clear ears. I could see and label those comments for what they were.

I've never heard anyone in my community state, "No me gustan los negros. Odio a los negros." *I don't like Black people. I hate Black people.* It's never that direct.

More common are vaguer statements.

"No te metas con los negros. Son peligroso!" *Don't get mixed up with Black people. They're dangerous!*

"Gracias a Dios, no tienes el pelo negro de verdad." *Thank God you don't have real Black people hair.*

Even though there were no outright racist, Karen-like, N-word–dropping situations, the microaggressions still stung.

CHAPTER 14
African Faith

L iving away from home and exploring Black history, I began taking a closer look at Santería, the religion I was raised in. Latinos, both acquaintances and family, would always refer to it as the religion of *Los Negros*, but anything beyond that was a mystery to me. We cared for and tended to altars for African orishas, but I wasn't sure why. I was just a child following the path of Mami and Roberto.

The faith survived slavery through its merge with Catholicism. The slaves matched each orisha, a deity synonymous with God or Goddess, with a Catholic saint. For example, in Santería/Lucumí, Saint Lazarus represents the orisha Babalú-Aye, and Saint Barbara represents the orisha Shango. Therefore, if a Spaniard slave master passed a group of slaves praying to Saint Lazarus, it wouldn't raise any red flags.

As for the slaves' religion, the masters believed they had nothing to worry about. They had forcefully converted all the Africans to Catholicism—or so they thought. In reality, the slaves continued to practice the faith behind the masters' backs, thus preserving their original faith and culture.

I knew Santería came from Africa, but I didn't know that it stemmed from the Yoruba people in West Africa. The religion reached many Latin countries through the transatlantic slave trade. Countries all over Latin America, from Cuba to Brazil, have followers of this African faith.

The English language morphed upon its arrival to the Americas; for example the British English accent of the colonizers developed into the Boston, Atlanta, New Orleans, and New York accents. The Yoruba faith transformed in a similar way.

Depending on the country, the spelling of some orishas' names differs. Shango can also be spelled as Ṣàngó, Changó, or Xangô. Yemaya is also spelled Yemọja, Yemanja, or Iemanjá. Ritualistic practices vary here and there, but for the most part, they remain the same.

To be honest, Santería and the elders in the religion terrified me while I was growing up. Using some unfathomable sixth sense, the elders always knew what irresponsible antic I was up to, even before I committed it. By my teenage years, when my antics weren't so childlike, I steered clear of the members of the religion completely. Girl, I'd be damned if the Babalawo said something about my latest crush in front of my family, especially when many of my crushes were women and I wasn't comfortable talking about that yet.

Sometimes, after rhythmic drum-playing and singing, members became overwhelmed with the spirit. The intensity of their dance moves increased. They might cry, scream, speak in tongues, or hug. Some even took off running around the whole house. Everything about it scared me.

I was concerned for the woman dancing and weeping uncontrollably. I worried about the man sprinting around the house for no reason. I was afraid that whatever overcame them would find its way to me. Now, I see it for what it is. It's a feeling of electricity, a connection to your ancestors and love, a sense so strong it almost makes you dance out of your skin. It's therapy for whatever you may be going through at that point in life, like shouting in the Black-American church. It is so many things, it's almost indescribable. Now, I can see the beauty.

During cleaning rituals, Roberto and other members of the faith recited prayers and chants in an unfamiliar language. It wasn't English or Spanish, yet all the members understood it but me. It jarred every nerve in my body. Later on, through research and open conversations with my stepdad, I learned it was an African dialect. Yet again, I was blown to smithereens. How did Roberto —a man born in Cuba, an island colonized by Spain decades ago—know prayers, chants, and adages in an African tongue? As it turns out, many of the languages used in Santería are a mixture of Yoruba and other African tongues. My young self, who was frightened by the unfamiliar language around her, was now an adult aware of the language's origins. And it wasn't so scary after all.

During this self-reflective journey, I discovered a documentary called *They Are We*. In the film, a man records Santería songs, ceremonies, and dances in Cuba, and then travels all the way to West Africa to present the footage to different tribes. Their reactions sent hair-raising chills down my body.

"I thought these people were extinct," an elder said with tears in his eyes.

"These people were taken away hundreds of years ago. We never knew what became of them. We thought they were gone. I haven't heard this language since I was a kid. I thought this language, these people, no longer existed."

Most of the West African tribes recognized the Santería songs and dances recorded in a little Cuban town hundreds of miles away. Their reactions brought tears to my eyes.

Before the Black-history rabbit hole, before my Black self-discovery, the connection to my African heritage was a worn-down bridge, stretching from my soul to the motherland. After I watched *They Are We*, the bridge was rebuilt with sturdy cement pillars stuck deep into the earth for reinforcement. I felt a connection to Africa beyond the features from my Papi's DNA.

Upon their arrival in the Americas, most of the slaves' cultures, languages, and customs were beaten out of them. They were forced to leave every part of their heritage behind and assimilate into the masters' way of life. And yet, this religion miraculously survived slavery. Not only did it survive, but Africans can still identify it today. In West Africa, many continue to follow Santería or at least have knowledge of it. Discovering I was raised in a religion that defied all those circumstances lit a flame in my soul. It instilled an extra layer of strength in my bones.

I come from strength. I come from resilience. I am a child of African blood and a product of the African Diaspora.

CHAPTER 15

The Black Girl in the Room

This poor Armenian woman, bless her soul. This is all my fault. I knew better than to do this.

In the mirror, I saw the scene unfolding before me. Her hands were sprawled out, fingers woven wildly into my hair. In jerky, uneasy motions, she attempted to part my hair into sections. But every task was laborious.

It took her a full ten minutes just to complete a straight middle part along the back of my head, which usually took me one minute. I shouldn't have come here, I thought. This woman has never seen my hair type before. This woman doesn't know how to do Black hair.

The hair salon was five minutes away from my house in San Fernando Valley. I'd visited Black hairstylists before, but their salons were miles away, and I was in no mood to drive thirty-five minutes to West LA. Besides, all I wanted was a dye—no bleach or drastic color change, just a natural dark brown. Who could mess *that* up?

The bright burgundy I wore in high school never faded away. No matter how many times I dyed my hair back to its natural color, tiny burgundy highlights managed to seep through a few months later. During the summer months, sunrays caused the undertone to rise as well.

I was used to the chaos of hectic bathroom setups, trying to read directions in a miniature font, with plastic gloves and brown hair dye all over the place. But this time, I wanted to avoid that. My last DIY dye job left the bathroom sink, cabinets, and floor sprinkled with eternal brown stains. It was a travesty. From that day on, I swore to add no more pigments to the collection.

A salon down the street quoted me twenty-five dollars for the job. Twenty-five dollars and no hair-dye stains forever embellishing my bathroom? What a steal! So there I was, slumped in a chair, observing this woman as she feebly battled my curls. In the mirror I spotted her co-worker, a Mexican woman with long, straight hair dangling to her waist. She was snipping her client's ends while side-eyeing the parody occurring on my head. A slight smirk formed in the corner of her mouth.

She whispered to her client, "Mírala. Ella está luchando con ese cabello." *Look at her. She is fighting with that hair.*

Her client, a middle-aged man unmoved by the gossip, inquired, "Te gusta trabajar con ella?" *Do you enjoy working with her?*

"No me importa. No hablamos el mismo idioma, así que no tenemos que hablar." *I don't mind it. We don't speak the same language, so we don't even have to talk.*

As the two conversed, I reached for the brush in the hairdresser's hand. "I can help untangle if you want, love! That way, it'll be quicker and easier for you." And faster, I thought, so you can throw some brown dye on this hair and I can escape.

With a blank face, the Armenian hairdresser nodded and handed me the brush. At that moment, it became apparent that the woman didn't speak much English. After taking a deep breath, I continued the detangling process. I couldn't care less what language she spoke. Make your money, sis! I would've felt better, however, if she had been fluent in the language of Black hair care.

It's fine, I thought. All she has to do is slap some hair dye on this and I'll be out. She's not cutting or blow-drying. Once I detangle the rest, it'll all be over.

In the middle of my self-calming session, the hairdresser's co-worker cackled. "Jajaja! Mírala! Ella no puede trabajar con ese pelo malo. Ella perdió la pelea!" *Hahaha, look at her! She can't work with that bad hair. She lost the fight!*

The air around me thickened. Everything stalled as if I were in a slow-motion scene. The cars passing by outside the salon window, the rest of her sentence, and the blink of my eyes slowed to a sluggish pace. Did she just say *pelo malo*? Did she really think I wasn't Latina? I'd been in the room when Mita talked trash about someone in Spanish, and I'd heard the rude comments people made about my Afro-Latino family. I've been outraged, but fury can't even begin to describe how I felt now that I was in their shoes. I was no longer witnessing micro-aggressions toward the Black person in the room; I *was* the Black person in the room.

I whipped my neck around and said in Spanish, "Bad hair?! She needs to know how to brush everyone's hair! People pay for this hair. There are wigs like this 'bad hair.' Eat shit!"

In my entire life, Spanish had never left my mouth at such a speed. I didn't even know I was capable of such a response! For a moment, it was as if the world had gone black and all the Renovales DNA had come to light.

Eyes wide and mouth agape, she looked like she'd seen a ghost. Her client's eyes widened as well, but a big smile extended across his face as he chuckled slightly.

When the dumbfounded hairdresser finally blinked out of her trance, she said, "No quise decir eso..." *I didn't mean to say that...*

I can't recall what she said after that. I turned back to the mirror and continued to unknot my hair, ignoring her existence. My hairdresser didn't understand what had transpired, but she saw my expression, heard the volume of my voice, and sensed the apparent tension. She remained still as I brushed through the rest of the knots. After detangling my hair, I handed the brush back to her and pointed at the brown hair dye on the color chart. Then she timidly finished the process. A little over an hour later, I paid. Before leaving the salon, I took one more look at the Mexican hairdresser. A female client had replaced the male one. She was clipping her client's bangs with her eyes practically glued to the woman's hair, refusing to look at me. I shook my head and left the salon.

Every time I witness people utter rude comments in front of my Afro-Latino family, every time I hear stories of what Black people suffered in the past or suffer in the present, my mind conjures up all the things I would do in those situations. All the obscenities I would say. All the terrible Yelp reviews I would write. All the exposing social media posts I would create. And depending on the gravity, all the legal help I would seek.

I'd thought about all these concepts, but when I wound up in their shoes, all my ideas were thrown out the window. Everything stood still. Time froze. I said something to the Mexican woman at the salon, but thinking back, I should've let that ignorant woman have every piece of me. I should've stormed out of that salon and taken my money to a Black-owned establishment.

A couple of years ago, while living in LA, there were two occasions in which a non-Black friend said the N-word in my presence. Neither of these people were new friends. They both knew me, knew everything I stood for, everything I posted online, everything I lived and breathed. They knew me—or, at least, I thought they did. Despite all the "knowing" and all the friendship, nothing stopped them from saying the insulting word.

In both instances, my limbs froze. My neck stiffened. My breath got shallower. I thought, Did that person really just say that? Did they really just say that around *me*, of all people? I've known this person for a long time. Why did this just come out now? "Uncomfortable" doesn't even touch the way I felt. Tons of questions swam through my mind. Then ten minutes had passed, and I hadn't said anything.

Thinking back, I should've addressed the issue then and there. I should've asked my "friends" what the hell was wrong with them. Maybe I should've popped them straight in the jaw; that could've been what came to mind the next time they thought it was okay to say. There were so many things I could've said or done, but the moment passed, and I did nothing.

CHAPTER 16

Why Did He Wanna Know So Much About Papi?

I don't remember where Mami picked me up from. The sky was darkening into the late evening. Mami's shoulders and chest slumped toward the steering wheel, her tired eyes focused on the road ahead. Her comfortable "home clothes" hung from her body while I sported a leotard, tights, and sweatpants.

After a day of school, I'd attend dance practice until nine o'clock at night. During this time, Mami worked a full-time job as a medical assistant at an OB-GYN's office. She left for work at seven in the morning, clocked out at five, picked us up from daycare, and continued the long day by transporting us to dance practice or to baseball practice with RJ.

The household duties were to be completed during a small window before bedtime. Roberto helped as much as he could, but his days as a sanitation worker were also demanding. His shifts began so early during the week, he'd be up and out of the house by three in the morning. Life's responsibilities were split between Mami, Roberto, and an eighteen-year-old Windaly. Still, the bulk of them inevitably fell onto Mami's shoulders.

Most days, Mami was just exhausted. In addition to her dense workload, she also unknowingly suffered from depression and the initial stages of an autoimmune disorder called multiple sclerosis. She wouldn't be officially diagnosed until about two years later, but doctors suspected she suffered from it as early as 2003.

From the passenger side of the car, I watched the road with her. I talked about the day's events, hoping to make the car ride pass more quickly. We were cruising down a desolate road in Town 'n' Country at a speed below the legal limit when we began to pass a large plaza, filled with a movie theater, nightclub, and multiple restaurants. We had barely covered ten feet before we heard a loud *whoop whoop!* I turned around to see blue and red lights.

After muttering some Spanish obscenities under her breath, Mami pulled the car over to a complete stop. With the police cruiser's high beams piercing our vision, we were unable to see the officer until his tall, Caucasian frame appeared at my mother's window. Mami adjusted in her seat to assume her best posture and rolled down the window.

"Hello, ma'am. Do you know why I stopped you?"

When working in a professional or English-speaking environment, a lot of minorities use a specific tone of voice.

For example, if an unknown number called Mami's phone, she'd answer with a formal, overly enunciated, "Hello, this is Windy speaking. May I ask who is calling?" She'd exaggerate her *t* and *s* sounds, bantering at a pace that was almost slow enough to conceal her accent.

Growing up, hearing this identity switch tickled every

bone in my body. I referred to the unfamiliar tone as her "White voice." But instead of answering a strange phone call or working at the doctor's office, Mami was now using this voice to communicate with the police officer.

"No sir, I do not," she replied.

"Your taillight is out, ma'am. Did you know this?"

"Yes, sir, my husband is going to fix it this weekend when we are off from work. He ordered the new light. It is supposed to arrive soon."

The officer paused, studying my mother's clothes, her facial expressions. Then his investigative glance moved to me.

After a moment, he released a small breath. "All right, ma'am. You get that fixed soon, please. I'll let you off with a warning. Have a good night."

"Yes, sir, I will. Thank you."

It was nothing like getting pulled over with my father years ago.

* * *

In the heart of TC, next to my neighborhood, is a larger community named Twelve Oaks. It has multiple entrances and exits. If we drove past one gate on Waters Avenue, an entrance at the next intersection on Hanley Road was at our disposal. In fact, there are about three different ways to enter Twelve Oaks from Hanley Road.

My family was well versed in using shortcuts to beat traffic on the main roads. My childhood self swore to keep this a secret, but I quickly learned that my family were not the only TC residents with this information. Many people made shortcuts through Twelve Oaks.

RJ's Little League field sat on the outskirts of the community. On sunny afternoons after baseball games, most game attendees—the mothers, fathers, coaches, and kids—departed by taking a swift right turn into Twelve Oaks instead of waiting at the intersection on Hanley Road. Everyone used the not-so-secret shortcut, including Papi.

One afternoon, when I was about nine, Papi and I were driving down Hanley Road. I'd spent most of the day with him; we ran errands, saw friends of his, and spent a lot of time at the Colombian bakery because he knew one of the customers. *Pan de bono and empanadas* pushed our stomachs to capacity. Now, it was time to take me home.

We were cruising down the street when Papi pressed the brake and turned right into Twelve Oaks. After making numerous turns, our car was several yards away from the exit when we heard a *whoop whoop!* Sirens rang in the air. A police car was pulling us over. For as long as I can remember, I've been afraid of the police. I don't know why, or where I learned that from, but they make me anxious. As an adult, I've noticed many minority children share the same, almost innate fear.

My attention turned to the front of the car. I took a deep breath in the back seat. A few moments later, a round-bellied police officer approached the window.

"Hello, sir. Do you know why I stopped you?"

"No, I don't," Papi said.

"Ran right through the stop sign back there. You didn't brake long enough. You're supposed to come to a complete stop and then continue driving."

"Oh, okay. I'm sorry," Papi politely replied.

After asking for his license and registration, the officer continued, "Where do you live?"

"5555 Drury Lane."

"Where are you going?"

"Taking my daughter back to her mom's house."

I assumed the officer would move on to writing a ticket, but he started asking strange questions. "Why are you driving through this neighborhood? Where do you work? Where were you born? Where does your daughter live? Is she really your daughter?"

The officer even shifted his gaze to ask me the same. "Young lady, is this your daddy? How old are you?"

After the not-so-short interrogation, the officer wrote Papi a ticket and warned him to be more careful next time.

For the next few days, I revisited the incident in my mind. I thought about my automatic anxiety the moment I heard the sirens. I began inventing some questions of my own. "Where do *you* work? Why does *that* matter? What?! Of course, I'm his daughter. Why did you ask Papi that? Why are you asking so many questions? Why do you need to know so much about Papi?"

CHAPTER 17

Excerpts from my Journal

When I was little, my cousin Dayanara had two hamsters. One slept in the far corner of its cage most of the day, ignoring our attempts to disturb its sleep. The other hamster almost never slept. It seemed to spend twenty-three hours a day running in endless circles on the hamster wheel. The hamster ran as fast as its little feet could manage, and the wheel spun and spun.

At first, the sight entertained me. Its little legs looked so stinking cute moving at such high speeds. But after a few days, the wonder wore off. I grew concerned about the hamster's well-being, to a degree beyond my young years. I wondered why the hamster ran so much. Did it lack substantial exercise? Did the confines of the tiny cage make it go mad? How could it board the wheel time and time again, knowing exactly what the outcome would be?

Being Black in America often feels like I'm a hamster on that wheel. But the wheel I'm running on is broken up into the five stages of grief: denial, anger, bargaining, depression, and acceptance.

The thought of twelve-year-old Tamir Rice being shot immediately after police arrived on the scene grips my heart to this day. And it was all because Tamir, a little Black boy, was playing in the yard with a toy gun in his hands.

Waiting seventy-four days for the arrests of William Bryan, Travis McMichael, and Gregory McMichael left me spinning in denial. I knew the justice system had its faults, and I was aware that Black Americans received the short end of the stick most of the time. But I couldn't believe their crime was caught on tape, that video went viral, and yet no arrests had been made. I couldn't believe it. There was no way the system could fail us that terribly.

Fury filled my veins when I read the online comments justifying Breonna Taylor's murder because she'd dated a drug dealer in the past. *Dated* a drug dealer. *In the past*. If that information wasn't accessible, the least they could've done is arrive at the correct home. I don't care if her mother and grandmother were drug dealers; that's an issue for the courts to address. The police aren't meant to be the judge, jury, and executioner.

On a few occasions, I tried to bargain with the truth. I thought, Maybe he shouldn't have talked back. Maybe he shouldn't have raised his voice. But I was quickly reminded of the numerous times police officers have dealt with uncomplying White people when the outcome, miraculously, wasn't death.

Sometimes, it felt like no amount of protesting or petition-signing could ever fix this, which depressed me greatly. When one battle was won, it seemed like five would be lost. Politicians and public figures announced their condolences with polite words, but it was nothing more than a Band-Aid on the real issues at hand—just a few polished words to hold us over until next time.

And eventually, despite all those feelings, we do what we do best: continue. I remain prayerful for my people and our spirits. I hope for change for my future children and their children. Amid all the chaos on social media, I make it my goal to showcase Black joy on my platforms—pure, talented, boisterous, Black joy. I'm the little hamster on that wheel, continuing.

* * *

The following entries are pure, unfiltered thoughts from my journal. I apologize for the profanity, and I apologize if this chapter perturbs you.

But I do not, in any way, shape, or form, apologize for my feelings. Sometimes the road toward understanding isn't easy. But I'm here today, writing about this with a level head, because of this path. And to my non-Black friends: take a breath, step outside yourself as much as you can, and keep reading. You might be offended; you might not. Good luck.

May 26, 2020

Hearing a grown man, a grown-ass man, become so scared, so frightened, he starts calling out for his momma? That shattered my heart. Rest in peace, George Floyd.

. . .

May 30, 2020

People who have the audacity to say Breonna Taylor's death was her fault make me sick to my stomach. I think I need to take a break from social media today. I still think about victims like Sandra Bland, Tamir Rice, and Trayvon Martin. I'm still trying to recover from seeing life leave Ahmaud Arbery's body after he was HUNTED. We are still fighting for them. How is God allowing more people to be added to this list?

May 31, 2020

Mami told me RJ is going to a baseball camp in rural Alabama this summer. He will train, eat, sleep, and work there for about four weeks. She said the area is so country, the nearest grocery store is twenty-five minutes away. Nothing but land, houses, and trees.

I didn't tell Mami what I was thinking because she shouldn't worry, but what the %@*#?! Racial issues have always been around, but this pandemic has forced everyone to pay attention. There are even international protests about the racial issues in America! The air is tense. White people everywhere are either waving Confederate flags, announcing their support to the Black community, silently watching from the sidelines to avoid ruffling feathers, or at home having heated debates with opposing family members. I don't wanna be pessimistic, but why do we think it's a good idea to send RJ to Alabama, alone, for the whole summer?

RJ is young. He's in high school. More importantly, he still hasn't left the Town 'n' Country bubble—the "we are all Cuban, Puerto Rican, or Dominican, and we don't see color" bubble. Does he know that bubble doesn't exist in other places? Does he know he's a Black boy and not like his White Latino friends? Lord. I need to pray.

June 6, 2020

Do I even want to have kids? Girlllll, I'm playin'. I've wanted to be a mom since I was twelve. But seriously, this world is crazy!

June 8, 2020

Honestly, the dance industry needs to get their $#*! together. I've been to so many auditions where White girls are separated into three categories: blondes, brunettes, and redheads. Meanwhile, Black people, Latinos, and Asians are clumped together. I'm really tired of people hiring light-skinned, mixed-race girls to check off the "Black" box. Instead of seeing different shades of chocolate, I'm looking at two girls that look exactly like me, an Asian girl, and a sea of White.

People continue to hire and fetishize mixed-race women. It makes me feel like we're the easier pill to swallow. We look exotic, we have Black features, but we aren't *too* Black. I should be seeing my dark-skinned sisters next to me at work. I should be seeing more dark-skinned women on jobs in general, and not just the ratchet twerking jobs.

· · ·

June 14, 2020

I'm kinda tired of White people asking me if I'm okay. I am okay. I'm more than okay—I feel great! I feel great knowing y'all are leading these protests, y'all are standing up to your family members, y'all are hitting the streets despite the tear gas and rubber bullets being hurled at you for peaceful protests. Step into a *piece* of our shoes and pay attention to how it feels. Videos are going viral of people infiltrating protests on purpose, looting and making terroristic threats. Remember what the government program COINTELPRO did to tarnish the Black Panther movement? I'm A-okay! You know when I wasn't? When I talked about these things in 2015 and y'all graciously ignored me and all my Facebook posts, but liked and commented when I posted about a dance job. I wasn't okay when y'all asked, "iS iT rEaLly aBoUt RaCe?"

Girlllll. Don't ask me if I'm okay. I feel great. I feel like I'm no longer screaming in a stadium packed with people who can't hear me.

June 30, 2020

I love that social media is around to show us things that might've never gotten attention.

September 10, 2020

The N-word.

When non-Black people are confronted about using the N-word, I will never understand why one of the most common responses is "Honestly, nobody should say it!"

That sounds like "Well, if I can't say it, nobody can!" Like an adult version of a tantrum, and privilege at its finest. How do you feel so comfortable telling a group of people what to do with a word—a word they took back?

"Hey! Jewish community! Shabbat dinners should actually take place on Tuesday instead of Friday!" I'm not Jewish, and I have no idea what their culture is like. So why would I say that? Oh yeah, I wouldn't, because that's dumb.

Should the word be uttered or not? How about you just stop saying it and let the Black community handle that? It does not concern you. In layman's terms, mind your business.

When non-Black people say, "I only said it when I was mad"... What?!

"My Black boyfriend lets me say it." Ma'am, your boyfriend is crazy, too.

"I was just singing a song!" Skip over the word like my niece when she sings songs with curse words.

"I grew up around Black people!" The Black people you grew up with who let that mess slide don't represent all the Black people in America. So if you get effed up, you get effed up. Don't say you didn't know.

I'm blown away by non-Black people's inability to relinquish the word without a fight. Why do you feel so comfortable using a word that isn't from your culture anyway? People let go of other insensitive words just fine. What's the deal with this one?

September 29, 2020

I am never, ever going to code-switch again. Forget

trying to make non-Black people comfortable. Forget over-enunciation and forced articulation. From now on, everybody and they momma are gon' get every piece of me and this hood Florida vernacular. I don't care how things are pronounced. Ion care if it's "draws" or underwear cause guess what? You can still understand me. Ion care about "sounding intelligent" because guess what? Using "I don't" or "Ion" aren't indicators of my intellect. I can speak in Ebonics, Spanglish, or straight-up curse words (as long as kids aren't around). Why? Because I turned on my TV to watch the first presidential debate tonight, and these two old-ass White men were on this TV acting *ghetto*. Yelling, talking over each other, being downright messy—it was ratchet! I felt like I was watching a *Bad Girls Club* reunion. No class, no self-control, no composure.

Why did I spend a great deal of my student life trying sooooo hard to make sure I sounded smart to White dance moms? Girl! The potential presidents of our country just got on TV and acted like buffoons, and I'm still trying to come off as a "smart" Black/Brown person in a room full of White people?! %@*# that. I hate that I felt the need to do that to begin with.

October 3, 2020

A lot of big corporations are putting in the work to be considered supportive and inclusive. They're all like, "Here at Bobo's store, we stand with Black lives."

In an ad for a big makeup store, there are four dark-brown Black people pictured. That's three more than the usual token. A few months ago, a lot of companies wouldn't have even used a dark-skinned girl. They would've selected a mixed person, checked the diversity box, and called it a day. Four dark-skinned Black people? That's beyond my wildest dreams!

While I admire all this Black love and inclusivity, it's long overdue. And I worry that these companies might be doing it to save face, throwing a few extra Black people in there so they don't get dragged on social media. People are being ripped to shreds left and right. It's a bloodbath. They look like they stand in solidarity on the outside so that they don't lose money on the inside. I pray that is not the case.

February 28, 2021

Windaly: I hate the phrase *pelo malo*. Why can't you just say "tighter curls"?

Me: Ugh, I can't stand that phrase.

Windaly: I've heard, "Wow, Taavi's hair is beautiful. When Windaly has a girl, watch her come out with *pelo malo*."

Me: What?! Who the %@*# said that?!

Windaly: Aunt Blah Blah Blah.

My family is wild. Things like that make me wish I still lived in Tampa. At this stage in my life, I'm pointing out all the mess, whether you're family or not. I know most of this is learned; it's their upbringing, so it might be challenging to unravel. I'm not even trying to get into long, heated arguments or unwind generations of racism. I just want to be there. I wanted to be there to turn to her and say, "Aunt Blah Blah Blah, you can't say that. You're grown. You're my family. I can't control what you say or don't say, but I can make sure you don't say that around me, my Black-ass nephews, my Black-ass brother-in-law, his Black-ass niece, my Black-ass wife, and my future Black-ass kids."

And I wouldn't even say "ass" cause that's my elder, and I'm still respectful. I'ma pray for that generation.

CHAPTER 18

A New Bih

Non-Black people, if you come by a term or
phrase that stumps you, google it. Learn
about other cultures. Black and White
Americans are part of the same country,
but there are still cultural differences.
Educate yourself on them; then Black
culture might not feel so foreign.

I wonder what it must've been like for my family to witness my Black discovery, to see the shift in my interests, to read my Black Power social media posts. What was it like observing the hip-length box braids swaying from my scalp the first time I visited home? I might have looked like I was trying to be "a new bih."

Braided hairstyles aren't taboo in my family. When she had the time, Mami braided everyone's hair. Before styling it into two-strand twists or six plaits for the week, she soaked our curls in rich oils and leave-in conditioner. She said it was a treatment for pelo seco, *dry hair*.

Once RJ's and Roberto's hair grew long, they had cornrows. Mami proved knowledgeable in curly-hair care, but braiding to the scalp wasn't her area of expertise, so the men got their braids done at the local barbershop every couple of weeks. I even went there from time to time. I attended my fifth-grade banquet with half my head in cornrows and the other half in roller curls. Nobody batted an eye then. But the world ceased to rotate when I showed up in Tampa at nineteen with box braids.

"Pareces como una negra," Mami said. *You look like a Black girl.*

"Ten cuidado con esos peinados de negras. Vas a perder tu pelo," Papi warned. *Be careful with those Black-girl hairstyles. You're going to lose your hair.*

"Y ese mapo?!" Mami asked. *And what is that mop?!*

Box braids were basically the cousin of my childhood hairstyles. But instead of six plaited braids or two-strand twists, a sea of braids poured from my scalp. My hair no longer sat at just a few inches past my shoulder; with the help of extensions, it flowed back and forth along my hips. Box braids weren't that different. Why did everyone have something to say about it?

Sometimes, my family entertained my Black discovery. They started talking about Afro-Latinidad more often. Suddenly, Roberto felt the need to open up to me about his dance styles, ones I'd seen him perform since I was little, with the kitchen or living room as his stage.

During one of my visits, Roberto broke down different Afro-Cuban movements: "This is Guaguancó. That is rumba." He explained how the slaves introduced each dance style to Cuba and how they remained relevant today. Roberto also introduced me to other Afro-Cuban musical artists. Los Muñequitos de Matanzas became one of my favorites. Papi talked about Chocó, Colombia, in closer detail. He reminisced about his upbringing and described life in the predominantly Black region of Colombia.

Mami also addressed Afro-Latinidad more often. She shared information about Afro–Puerto Ricans. She got me hooked on a telenovela called *Celia*, a show about *La Reina de la Salsa*, the Queen of Salsa—Afro-Cuban star Celia Cruz. I'd loved her since I was a kid, so when the *novela* came out, Mami made sure to call me. My wife and mother-in-law also adored the show.

The first few episodes left me breathless. I hadn't realized it before, but I'd never seen so many Afro-Latinos on a single Spanish platform! When I was younger, Afro-Latinos were only sporadically featured on networks such as Telemundo or Univision. I never saw people who looked like Papi or Roberto on TV. I never saw people like my Tia Mayra or my cousins Dayanara and Dayana. I never saw that piece of me on the screen.

While watching *Celia*, I daydreamed about all the Afro-Latino families, across all the seas, sitting at home tuning into the show. My heart lit up when I thought about the Afro-Latino children and teens seeing themselves on TV. There they were, not cast as the token, a slave, or a supporting role, but starring in the show as the main character. I imagined what it would've felt like to be represented in the media as a child. I finished the entire eighty-episode series in about three weeks.

Sometimes, I wondered if coming into my Blackness rubbed my Puerto Rican family the wrong way. I didn't want them to feel less loved or think I was less proud to be Puerto Rican. Culturally, I've always felt more Puerto Rican than Colombian, and I believe it has a lot to do with the inconsistency in my relationship with Papi. He moved in and out of our lives too much.

Being surrounded by Mami and the rest of my Puerto Rican family shaped my cultural identity. A lot of them lived in Tampa, and we took numerous trips to see our family on the island as well. Mita and Papito were the only grandparents I knew as a kid. Puerto Rican food, customs, and vocabulary molded me. My ears favored the *Boricua* accent because I understood it better; outside of Papi and Luz Marie, I had little practice with the Colombian dialect. Papi didn't have a lot of family in Florida, and I never visited Colombia. I just felt more Puerto Rican.

A few years into my adulthood, after I had moved to LA, I visited my White Puerto Rican family and discussed Afro-Colombian this, slavery that, and *racismo* in American and Latino culture. That was probably a big jump for my family.

There is a documentary on Amazon Prime entitled *Little White Lie* about a biracial woman named Lacey Schwartz, who grew up believing she was White. She had Jewish parents yet arrived into the world with caramel skin, full lips, and big, curly hair. Her family often attributed her features to a Sicilian paternal grandparent. In due course, she uncovered the family secret: her mother had an affair with a Black man. Throughout the film, Lacey shares her stories, the effect of her confused upbringing, and her journey of Black discovery.

One of the most memorable moments was when she orchestrated a small reunion with her college friends. They laughed, sipped wine, reminisced, and eventually discussed Lacey's Black discovery. Somehow, the topic of biracial identity arose. She wondered, Am I Black? Am I White? Am I both? Do I pick a side? There's the infamous one-drop rule: one drop of Black blood, and you're Black. Do I abide by that?

Lacey said she preferred to identify as a Black woman. She liked being a part of the Black community; it felt good, and it was easier to be accepted by them. One friend said that although it was more comfortable to identify as Black, she believed it was important to simultaneously identify as White: "There is power in forcing White people to accept you as part of their community."

That quote stays with me to this day. There is power in staring an all-White community in the face and declaring, "I am White. Whether you like it or not, I am a part of you." It reiterates the fact that White people cannot disassociate themselves from someone just because of Black DNA. It's meant for those who tell biracial people, "Oh, you aren't *really* Black," or, "You're not *that* Black." It's meant for those non-Black Latinos who turn up their noses and criticize dark-skinned Afro-Latinos, yet somehow adore my light-skinned guts. It's intended for those who don't think about their one or two Black friends when racially motivated crimes occur in our country.

Standing in your Blackness while identifying as both says, "Yes, regardless of my mixed race, I am Black. Philando Castile, Sandra Bland, and Trayvon Martin could have easily been my family or me."

For the mixed-race kids who fall on the Blacker end of the spectrum—my chocolate, 4A–C curly mixed kings and queens identifying as both—you can reiterate, "Yes, I am White. I am part of you, no matter what I look like on the outside. You cannot disconnect from me."

A lot of my dark-skinned mixed friends often vent about feeling displaced while being in predominantly white spaces. They often feel like the Black elephant in the room. I've felt like the "other" when Mami's side of the family has commented about my hair or the resemblance to my "ugly" father. I wondered how I could resemble my ugly father, yet somehow not be ugly. This led me to also wonder why my hair didn't lie down like theirs. Why did it frizz so much when it dried, and why was it so unruly? As a teen, I used record-breaking amounts of gels and hairsprays to keep my curls suppressed by gravity. But it always ended in a crunchy, frizzy mess. I wanted the soft Jessica Alba waves with all my might.

During one scene in *Little White Lie*, Lacey recalled how she felt in the Black community. She felt welcomed. She felt accepted. People no longer questioned her looks. Her dark skin was now light skin, and nobody cared what complexion she was. She said it felt good to be Black. By the end of that scene, thick tears were streaming down my face. That was precisely how I felt.

In Town 'n' Country, Caribbean accents rang heavily in my ears. Thick Dominican, Jamaican, Cuban, and Puerto Rican dialects filled the air. The hypnotizing smells of their cuisines made my mouth water.

A great deal of our family spoke English, but when the language wasn't necessary, Spanish flowed from their mouths. It was the primary language at home. It was also the language spoken throughout my neighborhood.

The dance studio where I trained for long hours after school, my second home, had a different atmosphere. English was the primary language, but Spanish floated around from time to time. Latinos were the majority, White people came in second, and there weren't many Black people or Asians. During all my years there, I recall training alongside just a couple of Black or Asian dancers.

In TC, I was accustomed to interacting with first-generation kids like myself. Our parents barely spoke English, and we communicated with them in the tongues of our home countries. Whether it was fluent or broken, we all spoke Spanish. There were a handful of first-generation kids at the dance studio, but the majority were second- and third-generation. For a lot of those kids, English was the only language spoken at home. It was common for their parents, grandparents, aunties, and uncles to be fluent in English. These types of Latinos intrigued me since they were unlike my "straight off the boat" family. These Latinos seemed to adapt to American culture like it was an effortless dance.

As a teenager, I categorized these people as "Americanized Latinos." They teetered between Latino and American, but they often, according to my pubescent logic, felt more American than Latino. No trace of an accent could be detected. If it wasn't for their olive skin tones or last names like Sanchez, Alvarez, and Rodriguez, they could've passed for White Americans.

Many Latina dance moms were married to White-American men, thus allowing the women to pass as Americans with their new last names. Their children went to private schools, wore brands I considered high-end at the time, like Tory Burch, and even listened to American music with their families. Imagine the culture shock when I witnessed a Latina friend belt out a Taylor Swift song with her mother, word for word. Before meeting my studio friends, I didn't have the slightest clue who Taylor Swift was. Local Tampa artists like Strizzo and Tampa Tony filled my MP3 player.

"Happy Birthday to You" and a couple of Celine Dion tracks are probably the only English tunes my mother and I could perform together.

There was a lot Mami didn't know, but American music wasn't totally foreign to her. She spent a few of her teenage years in Tampa, so old-school music always jump-starts memories from Jefferson High. Cyndi Lauper, Kool & the Gang, and Stevie B hold special places in her heart. But after that era, she stopped following American music. Artists like La India, Héctor Lavoe, Willie Colón, and Marc Anthony are the only greats that graced the speakers at family parties. From time to time, often by Roberto's hand, some nineties hip-hop or electronic track slipped in. But for the most part, salsa, merengue, and bachata reigned.

Instead of *arroz con gandules, pasteles, pernil,* or other Hispanic dishes, the party food provided by my Americanized Latino dance friends included fruit-and-cheese plates, hamburgers, hot dogs, and pita and hummus. They introduced many new flavors to my palate. Until then, I had no idea what hummus was! Though it originated in the Middle East, preteen and teenage Yoyi considered it a White-American dish. Cheese and fruit were odd on my taste buds, but it was a delightful change from the almost daily servings of *arroz con habichuelas.*

In Town 'n' Country, many followed the hustle-and-bustle way of life. It was typical to see a man cutting hair out of his garage, someone selling *coquito*—a Puerto Rican holiday drink—for extra income, or an older woman like Mita sewing and doing taxes out of her home. Others had hands-on jobs and worked as electricians, truck drivers, or contractors.

Before being diagnosed with MS, Mami was a medical assistant, and Roberto was a sanitation worker. Their jobs weren't the highest tier, but they were essential; they made the world go round. The dance studio, however, introduced me to a whirlwind of occupations.

"Your dad's a CEO? What's that?"

"Your mom made her money from stocks? Is that like the lottery?"

"Your mom doesn't work cause your dad owns four McDonald's franchises? What's a franchise?"

Career paths I'd never even thought of made themselves known to me. I studied the shiny, brand-new vehicles that dropped off dancers and compared them to the older, bulky white Astro van Mami drove. The van was large, loud, and reliable. It transported my family all over Tampa for over twenty years. We nicknamed the car "the Great White."

Outside of their leotard and tights, my classmates dressed in expensive Hollister and Abercrombie & Fitch. I knew of the brands, but Mami never stopped in those stores. Instead, she bulldozed past them, hunting for the bargain stores at the mall. My future wardrobe lived on the racks of Ross, Rainbow, and maybe JCPenney *if* they were having a sale. Parents and children reminisced about the summer, when they had vacationed at their beach homes or took a trip to the Florida Keys. Meanwhile, my mind froze at the idea of owning two homes.

When I was around thirteen years old, Mami allowed me to attend a few sleepovers hosted by some classmates. Before, there were only three places I could spend the night: my cousin Dayanara's house, my cousin Karol's place, and my best friend Elizabeth's house. Elizabeth was the exception to the "only family" rule because her father worked out of town and wasn't home for weeks at a time.

My teenage brain couldn't comprehend why that mattered, but I respected my mother's rules. At the sleepovers outside of my family's and Elizabeth's houses, more differences between myself and my studio friends came to light.

Town 'n' Country wasn't Beverly Hills, but it wasn't the hood either. Some homes were new with spacious land and beautiful yards sprouting short, bright-green grass. Other homes were more worn, with overgrown yards and fading exterior paint. Some shopping centers boomed with sales and vibrant consumers. Others were decorated with "For Sale" signs and remained vacant for months. Trader Joe's and Whole Foods were nonexistent, but the neighborhood *mercado*, market, and Walmart sufficed. The demographic was mostly Latino, with few Black or Asian people and an even smaller percentage of White people—or, at least, that's what it felt like. Some would consider TC part of Tampa's working class or lower working class.

Most of my dance friends lived in more affluent Tampa suburbs, like Westchase, Carrollwood, and Lutz. Their homes belonged to newer communities with protocols meant to uphold the neighborhood's integrity, such as maintaining a clean-cut yard and neutral colors. Whole Foods and Trader Joe's were down the street. White people were often the majority.

New cars, like Mercedes, Audi, and BMW, filled the driveways instead of the 1996 Honda Civic typical in TC. Inside their homes, everything functioned just as it should. There was no alternative way to turn on the faucet or TV. At home, our shower handle had to be turned in the most delicate fashion; otherwise, the handle detached from the wall. Their showers turned on without hassle and the water heated up effortlessly, no matter how many were using it. In the Renovales-Apolinario-Gutierrez household, if everyone had to shower, only the first two people would be lucky enough to bask in soothing hot water. After that, trembling cold showers were in store for the rest of us. For some reason, after about twenty minutes, the hot water just ran out. Pools and hot tubs transformed my friends' backyards into miniature water parks. Our yard had just enough space for a four-by-four-foot garden, which we filled with a small grill, a storage shed, and Roberto's altar. A seemingly endless supply of food was available in their refrigerators and pantries. Each time fresh groceries made it to my home, my siblings and I ravaged them within two or three days.

Enrolling in that dance studio jump-started one of the first culture shocks in my life. Before that, I was under the impression that new homes, white picket fences, and nice cars were strictly a *gringo*, White-American, phenomenon. I didn't know Latinos thrived in the realm of the American Dream.

From my sheltered perspective, all Latinos lived like my family. We worked hard to get by, mostly spoke Spanish, and didn't experience many of the finer things in life. Owning multiple properties, traveling abroad to places other than our home countries, paying tuition for K–12 education—those things were destined for *gringos*. When I saw Latinos experiencing these luxuries, it rattled me, but it also excited me. Latinos *can* achieve the American Dream, I thought. We didn't have to toil to survive.

In other ways, observing these Americanized Latinos concerned me and raised many questions. A lot of them didn't speak Spanish, but they still prided themselves on being Cuban. So-and-so said she didn't teach her children Spanish because her American husband wasn't comfortable not understanding what they were talking about. Why couldn't he have learned with them? Wasn't he aware that bilingual people are more likely to be hired? How did that dance mom, who barely spoke English, date older White men with high-paying professional careers? Was she doing it on purpose? Why did they feel more American than Latino?

Although the queries plagued me, I focused on the lessons I could learn from these Latinos. Much of my upbringing revolved around Puerto Rican culture, but there will forever be a few pieces of the puzzle missing—pieces only those who grew up on the island could claim. I was born in the States. My Spanish was limited. I didn't think I was as Americanized as some of my dance mates, but I wasn't on the same level as my cousins who were born and raised on the island. Instead, I was swimming in the middle of the spectrum between Americanized Latino and Puerto Rican native.

I stood by, observing all the different Latinos around me.

At the age of seventeen, taking all my experience into account, I made a silent pact:

No matter what, I will become fluent in Spanish. Not just fluent enough to carry out grocery store conversations or bank transactions, but enough to read in Spanish, write in Spanish, watch documentaries in Spanish, and thrive in Spanish-speaking countries, regardless of the dialect.

My children will speak Spanish. I'll surround them with Central American, South American, and Caribbean cultures so that they understand every dialect. (I would love to mingle with my Central American neighbors. Unfortunately, most of our interactions involve deciphering accents and differing words.)

I will make sure my future spouse accepts Spanish as a part of our life.

It's easy for culture to be erased among generations. Take me for example, a daughter of two Spanish-speaking parents who struggled to conjugate Spanish verbs. If I married someone who wasn't Latino, they would have to be okay with our children learning about their culture. There'd be no room for discomfort because we're speaking another language. In Europe, it's common for folks to speak different languages. Let's get with the program! Fortunately, my wife accepts my culture with open arms, every single part of it, and wants to raise bilingual children.

I will instill a connection between my children and our home country. We will make at least one visit per year, more if possible, to Puerto Rico or Colombia.

Many of the second- and third-generation kids I knew growing up had never visited their home countries! How are they supposed to feel Cuban or Dominican if they've never visited Cuba or the Dominican Republic? My children should have connections to their roots. Maybe I'll go as far as purchasing a vacation home there.

I will achieve the American Dream. Even though I presumed it was reserved for *gringos* and Americanized Latinos, this dream will be mine, and I will hold on to my culture while achieving it.

CHAPTER 19

Culture Shock

From kindergarten to the third grade, I attended an elementary school on the outskirts of TC called Crestwood Elementary.

Every morning, a miniature white-and-pink Hello Kitty alarm clock jolted me out of sleep. After peeling myself out of bed, I washed my face, brushed my teeth, and then staggered into Mami's room. By the time I entered with a brush and Luster's Pink Hair Moisturizer in hand, Roberto was long gone; his workdays started at three in the morning. After Mami had secured my hair into a ponytail or pigtails, her home hair salon was closed until the following day.

In the kitchen, I munched on some warm *pan Cubano con mantequilla*, Cuban bread with butter, accompanied by a *cafesito con leche*, coffee and milk—the breakfast of champions. Following *desayuno*, breakfast, I was escorted to the bus stop. Some days, Mami walked me, sporting her medical scrubs and comfortable work shoes. Once the bus arrived, she'd wave me off, blow me a kiss, and make her way to work.

Other days, Mita filled the position. About fifteen

minutes before the bus was scheduled to arrive, Mita left her house with a little bag of *papitas*, chips, in one hand and her house robe clutched in the other. She always blessed me with an extra snack to store in my book bag. One week it was *papitas*, the next it was Rice Krispies Treats, and the week after that it might be *galletas*, cookies. She'd walk two streets down and pick me up from Mami's house (my *abuela* lived within walking distance), and then we walked to the bus stop.

While we waited, she delivered her ritualistic instructions on how to *potarse bien*, behave well in school: "Mantente concentrada." *Stay focused.* "Quédate sentada." *Stay seated.* "Escucha la maestra." *Listen to your teacher.* "Si no entiendes algo, hacer preguntas." *If you do not understand something, ask questions.* If Christmas was around the corner, she might add, "Pórtate bien por que Santa Claus te está mirando." *Be good because Santa Claus is watching.*

After preparing and molding my young mind for the day, she gave me my *bendicion*, blessing. There were about ten other kids at the bus stop, and most of them received a *bendicion* before boarding. The neighborhood was Latino. The school was Latino. From the principal to the janitors, a tinge of an accent and a Latino surname were expected.

There were a few other races and ethnicities in the mix. My music teacher, Mr. Strawbridge, was a young Black man with charismatic energy and serious trumpet skills. I recall my chorus teacher being a Black woman. She ran a strict classroom but also had a little fun when the students behaved. Her relaxed, humorous side reminded me of the actress Jackée Harry from the show *Sister, Sister*. My guidance counselor was a petite older White woman with blond hair and tiny reading glasses that sat on the tip of her nose.

My kindergarten teacher, Mrs. Turner, had pale skin and black hair cut into a bob. But she explained that her great-grandmother was from Cuba, and Turner was her husband's name. Although she didn't speak Spanish, she was second-generation Cuban. By the time I was in third grade, my primary teacher was White American; I believe her name was Mrs. Bow. Her skin was olive-toned, and her wavy hair always swayed across her back. She was sweet as pie. Sometimes students took advantage of it, but she always wrangled them back in.

Despite flickers of other flavors, Crestwood Elementary was a lavish mixture of Caribbean flags. That's what I was accustomed to.

* * *

In the fourth grade, I attended Muller Elementary Magnet School. Located off 22nd Street and Fletcher Avenue, twenty-five minutes away from Town 'n' Country, Muller was in a primarily Black neighborhood. While walking through the halls or outside, I noticed the floors were cleaner than those at my last school.

Instead of crayon marks and old globs of gum stuck to the floor, I saw shiny, freshly mopped and waxed tiles. The concrete outside looked as if construction workers had laid it down the week before. I guessed that more money must pour into magnet schools because the cleanliness surpassed Crestwood's by light-years.

When Mami told friends or family members I was now

attending Muller, their first reaction was confusion: "Where is that?"

As soon as "the intersection of 22nd and Fletcher" left my mother's lips, their faces would scrunch up, they'd frown, or they'd combust into laughter.

"What? She goes to school out there?!"

"Isn't that a dangerous neighborhood?"

"Con los negros?"

"In the hood?"

"Isn't that a poor school?"

I was too young to comprehend the weight of their comments, but I did have questions. Who cared if I went to school with Black kids? Dangerous neighborhood, poor school? Muller was ten times nicer than my old school and had half the students! I received way more one-on-one attention there.

At Muller, Latinos weren't in the majority. The teachers were White or Black, with a few Latinos and Asians sprinkled in. The numbers may not have proved this, but it often felt as though the Black teachers were the majority. Perhaps they were, or maybe I came to that conclusion because I'd never seen so many Black professionals in one building.

I was sure of one thing: Muller Elementary had more Black students than my last school. I'd never seen or interacted with so many Black African-American boys and girls before. Of course, I had experienced that many Afro-Latino children, but there was a difference. For one, "Afro-Latino" was a term I didn't hear until my late teens or early twenties. According to my young logic and most of the adults around me, Black Latinos were categorized by their ethnicity before their race. Therefore, my Afro-Latina cousin Dayanara was

Cuban. Papi was Colombian. *Fulana*, what's-her-name, was Dominican. Everybody was anything but Black.

Although both African Americans and Afro-Latinos are African descendants, their cultures diverged and led to different outcomes. African-American culture was something I'd never seen before, at least not in detail. It came into my life like a whirling tornado of comparison, culture shock, and fascination. The Black children at Muller had innate manners; every adult was met with "yes ma'am, yes sir" or "no ma'am, no sir." A few students integrated obscenities into their vocabulary, but the Black students with outstanding manners stood out to me the most.

Occasionally, I'd heard Mami refer to her elders as *Señora* or *Señor*. Still, those instances were few and far between, almost as if the formalities forced upon her by Mita dwindled and were no longer a rule by the time my siblings and I came around. The main social rule Mami enforced was sitting still, calm, and collected in a friend or relative's home. She also loathed it when one of us asked for food at someone's house. If the host offered us food, and we accepted in a manner she deemed too eager, her right eye would twitch. She said it made her look like she never fed us. *Saludando*, greetings, were one of Mami's favorite social rules to enforce. If I walked into a party, said hello, but failed to kiss everyone on the cheek, I'd never hear the end of it. Everyone got a kiss, from my great-aunt to the infant in the stroller, no matter what. Mami favored her rules, but they never included "yes ma'am" and "no ma'am." Watching these kids with their conditioned manners was fascinating.

Years later, when I was about fifteen, I introduced my mother to my first girlfriend, Tominique, a Black American from Belmont Heights, Tampa, Florida. She also greeted my mom as "ma'am" or "Mrs. Windy." We dated for about three and a half years, and for all that time, she never stopped calling Mami "Mrs. Windy." And every time Tominique spoke to my mother with such formality, Mami's eyes twinkled, her chest swelled up, and a smile spread across her face. I guess manners excited her, too.

As a nine-year-old at Muller, I marveled at the countless braided hairstyles the Black girls wore. My experience with braids stopped at individuals, two-strand twists, and maybe half a head of cornrows to style the hair that'd been left out. But these girls wore an endless catalog of styles: box braids, beads, cornrows with patterns, and additional hair woven in. I absolutely loved it!

After fourth grade, and for the majority of my K–12 education, I continued to attend magnet schools in predominantly Black neighborhoods. The culture shock from elementary school subsided by the time I entered middle and high school.

* * *

I met Omar Brumley when I was about twelve. He was a dark-chocolate Black man straight from the South Side of Chicago. He and his New York–born wife, Jessica, lived in Tampa where their son Shabazz, played Little League Baseball with my brother.

When it came to expressing his beliefs and opinions, Omar never used the slightest impression of a filter. He had no qualms sharing his views on White America or discussing the realities of a Black man in a room where other Black-

American men were absent. When he explained that Shabazz wasn't born with the same freedom and liberties as a White boy, there was no trace of fear or hesitation in his voice. His tone was never argumentative or rageful; it was almost nonchalant. Still, some would categorize Omar as radical or militant.

Before Omar, most opinions I'd heard regarding White America were comical.

"No puedemos llegar tarde a este fiesta! Sabes que los gringos siempre llegan temprano!" *We can't be late for this party! You know White people always get to the party early!*

During one beach day, we witnessed a White dance dad slapping numerous burger patties on the grill, adding the world's tiniest pinch of salt, and then cooking them to a tough, tasteless finish. Salt? Just salt? Not even pepper, at least? Where's the garlic or onion powder? No *adobo* or *sazón*, marinade or seasoning? Throughout the ordeal, we shot looks of disbelief at one another. Most of us were trying to refrain from bursting into laughter.

Later that day, Mami brought the event up. Through stifled giggles, she noted, "Sabes que, los blancos cocinan diferente!" *You know, White people cook differently!*

When describing the Confederate flag–waving White people in small Florida towns, the adults around me used a more serious tone.

"Esos gringos están loco. Si estas manejando en sus pueblos, maneja rapido y salte volando!" *Those White people are crazy. If you're driving through their neighborhoods, drive fast and get the hell out of there!*

Whether the conversations were comical or somewhat solemn, they never lasted long. On the other hand, Omar could discuss all the layers of White America—the complex, the comical, and the flat-out corrupt—for hours upon hours, while maintaining the intellect of an HBCU graduate and the grit of a man from the South Side. Most of the time, he was cool and collected during these discussions. But sometimes, more passion and vigor arose. If his point fell on deaf ears, the volume of his voice intensified. Because he was often the only Black American present, a thin mist of frustration would cover him.

Most did not enjoy Omar's passionate conversations and the thick cloud of uneasy energy that formed around them. Some people were as passionate as him, but passionate about attempting to debunk his points. Others played conversational double-Dutch, tapping in and out. Many looked on as if Omar was a toddler throwing a tantrum. The majority seemed to label him as the combative, overly passionate Black man—otherwise known as the "angry Black man."

"*Dios mio!* I swear he thinks we are still in slavery!" Mami bellowed one afternoon following a get-together at Omar's house. "He just goes on and on like Black people are still in chains!"

Roberto chuckled and shrugged off his wife's miniature rant, like most mild-tempered husbands would. My siblings remained silent, continuing with whatever they'd been doing. But with wide eyes, I just observed my mother and her frustration with Omar's racial topic of the day. I didn't dare utter a word, but for some reason, I couldn't agree with my mother.

I wasn't a chocolate Black girl from the South Side of Chicago, but I was a biracial Latina in Tampa who noticed how differently Black people and those of lighter complexions were treated. In school, the "problematic" Black boys and girls were reprimanded as if they were adults. Meanwhile, teachers who dealt with challenging non-Black students could conjure up obscene levels of empathy.

I've sat like a deer in headlights while lighter-skinned family members trashed the appearance of a Black person. I was too young to understand the systematic racism Omar preached about, but something inside me still wanted to listen.

If racial inequalities were present in social and school life, why wouldn't they bleed over to career and political life as well? Racially motivated conversations aside, I introduced Omar so that we could get acquainted with the source of one of the later culture shocks in my teen life: affluent Black Americans.

I met many of my Black-American friends through magnet schools. Most of them lived in Black neighborhoods like Temple Terrace, Port Tampa, and Seminole Heights. Many lived in well-known low-income housing projects across the city: Robles Park, Belmont Heights, or the old North Boulevard community across from Blake High School, which was demolished in my adulthood. My middle school, Orange Grove Performing Arts, was in the center of Belmont Heights and Ybor City. This neighborhood was filled with renovated low-income housing, older homes, and a sometimes questionable crime rate.

On a few occasions, the school was placed on lockdown due to police activity in the neighborhood. Most of the time, though, I felt safe. Orange Grove had an excellent dance program, which I was lucky enough to fully participate in. We studied ballet, modern dance, and dance history. I was introduced to classics like *West Side Story*, *Cats*, Alvin Ailey's *Revelations*, and so many more. Some days our dance teacher, Mrs. Perkins, would put on urban dance films like *Rize*, or documentaries on the history of hip-hop.

These were my first introductions to Black-American styles of dance and folklore. The urban dance films were my personal favorites, but she only played them on free days, such as field day, exam day, and the last day of school.

By the time I reached seventh grade, Orange Grove had added a hip-hop team to their list of after-school programs. I was already a member of the lyrical/jazz program, but I stood first in line at the hip-hop team auditions. Around this time, the dance studio I was attending offered nothing outside of ballet, jazz, tap, and lyrical, so I was itching to get some hip-hop training.

After I made the team, my after-school schedule became quite rigorous. I spent Monday and Wednesday afternoons in a sea of jetés, pirouettes, and jazz. Tuesday and Thursday afternoons were filled with a lot of popping, locking, and dropping. Monday through Thursday, following practice at Orange Grove, Mami picked me up and took me to my ultimate obligation—the dance studio—where I rehearsed for the rest of the night.

For the most part, I would've categorized myself as a decent kid. Despite my hectic schedule, I maintained A's and B's on my report cards. I did my best to take every class seriously in tribute to the money Mami spent on tuition. I never hit that teenage milestone of disrespect, the "I hate you, Mom! No one understands me! I'm gonna run away!" phase many teens seem to go through.

Besides, Mami would've beaten that attitude straight out

of my behind the instant it reared its ugly head. But at the end of the day, I was still a teenager with the ability to make dumb decisions.

Like most sports, the dance teams at Orange Grove had seasons: certain months out of the year where regular practices took place. Ours were autumn and spring. It was our job as students to tell our parents the days and times of after-school practices. There was no teacher-parent communication, no weekly newsletter, and no emails. Therefore, I had to tell Mami to pick me up after dance practice from Monday to Thursday. In fact, I told Mami to pick me up after school all year, regardless of whether practice was scheduled or not.

During off-seasons, from the last school bell to 5 p.m., thirteen-year-old Yorelis could be found all over the Belmont Heights Estates housing community. Many of my friends lived there, as did a great deal of my crushes. I was living a totally secret after-school life. I rode on the handlebars of bicycles and sprinted in playgrounds. I discovered corner-store delicacies that were never to be found in Town 'n' Country; to this day, one of my all-time favorite bubblegums can only be found in a Belmont Heights corner store. I experienced slobbery first kisses at my boyfriend's house because his mother was never home, while at the same time—and confusingly—having my first girl crush on a close friend. Months later, I would explore that girl crush and develop my first feelings of teenage love.

From seventh to eighth grade, I lived a new, adventurous, and downright irresponsible life after school. And every day around 4:45 p.m., I walked back to Orange Grove, waited for my mom to arrive, and hopped into the car as if

I'd had a strenuous day of dance practice. (Mami, if you're reading this, I'm sorry! I can feel the spirit of a *chancleta* flying toward my rear end for even typing this.)

Careless and fun teenage antics filled my after-school schedule, but I was also being introduced to the "real world." After going to my boyfriend's house for the third or fourth time, I became concerned. Why was his mother never home? When I asked about her estimated time of arrival, he always replied, "I don't know." He explained that his mother's absence was ordinary. It was common for her not to come home for days.

I was dumbfounded. Did he cook? He said he didn't know how to cook. He either got some snacks from the corner store or boiled water for Top Ramen. Some days, his older brother stopped by. He'd check on his brother and the house, ask about their mother's whereabouts, and then leave. I also questioned how in the world he functioned being home alone so often. I hated being home alone. After one hour by myself in Mami's house, I was frantically looking over my shoulder for axe murderers. Eventually, the reality of my boyfriend's home life hit me: he was raising himself at thirteen.

Traveling around Belmont Heights, whether I was walking or riding on a friend's handlebars, I'd see many other children playing outside, from teenagers like myself to wobbling toddlers. I seldom interacted with the kids who didn't attend my school, but I felt their energy. They played tag, ran through sprinklers, and splashed around broken fire hydrants. They seemed so free, oozing with unrelenting joy.

In addition to that joy, however, I couldn't help but notice a few other details. Many of the frolicking children were shirtless, shoeless, or in diapers. Mami would've beaten me senseless if she caught me outside barefoot. They jumped on abandoned mattresses. Whenever balls catapulted out of their playing area, children chased them into the street without any regard for oncoming traffic.

Years later, while dating Tominique in high school, I would once again become a regular visitor to the Belmont Heights Estates, where she lived. On my way to her home one evening, I was twisting and turning all over Belmont Heights. When I was about two blocks away, a tiny but long-limbed Brown boy stumbled onto the road a short distance away from my car. I slammed on the brakes in a millisecond, causing the 1999 Honda Accord to rock forward.

With a racing heart and cold sweat forming in my armpits, I laid my eyes upon the kid. I knew the boy's life might have ended had I been going faster. Under the glow of the streetlight, I made out his mocha skin and expressive eyes. His gaze was frozen, also in shock. He wore nothing but sneakers and a pull-up diaper. His limbs were long, as if a growth spurt was expected. He couldn't have been any older than four.

Following our fleeting disbelief, he continued to cross the street. I scanned the surrounding buildings. What in the world?! Where were his parents? In the blink of an eye, I steered the car to the side of the road, turned the hazard lights on, and exited the vehicle in a sea of rage and bewilderment.

"Aye, little boy! Excuse me! Little boy!"

He stared at me with a blank expression.

"Where's your momma?"

His face was unshifting.

I paused, breathed deeply, and then reached out my hand. "Come with me."

His tiny fingers intertwined in mine, we crossed the street into the community. There were a small group of twelve-year-old boys playing football, but no adults were in sight. I asked if the boys knew this diaper-clad cutie and the whereabouts of his mother. They pointed me toward his house, which was another twenty feet away from the street he ran into. With my armpits still moist from nearly hitting the child moments ago, I located his mother at last.

For the next few days, this experience revisited me like a movie, playing most hours of the day. With every showing, I added to a list of unsettling details that I'd overlooked while focusing on finding the boy's mother. It took days for me to realize the group of boys playing football were outdoors, unsupervised, at around eight in the evening. It also took days to consider how fast they identified the mocha-toned mystery boy, almost as if it was common to see him out at that time. I couldn't help but wonder if it was also ordinary for the little boy to be unsupervised.

The most unnerving image was the dull expression on the boy's mother's face as the child and I walked up to the porch: she just stared blankly. There was no sense of concern, no panic regarding his whereabouts, and no questions about the stranger he just showed up with. She bore the same urgency as someone reading the Sunday newspaper and drinking a cup of tea.

"Hello, ma'am," I said. "Your son ran out into the street while he was playing. I wanted to make sure he got back home safely." I decided to leave out the part about almost hitting him with my car. Wouldn't want to frighten her.

She looked down at her son and, with as much emotion as a piece of coal, replied, "Oh. Well, boy, get back into the house."

Riddled with concern and confusion, I blurted out, "Um, well, good night..." Then I returned to my car.

This is going to make me sound sheltered and uneducated, but that's what I was: I believed that about 95 percent of African Americans lived similar or identical lives to the people in these stories, with extreme poverty, single-parent households, poor parenting, and violence being the norm. Until I was about nineteen, Omar and a handful of others were the only exceptions to this invented statistic.

Omar wasn't just the exclusion; it was more like he shot down my fabricated statistic with a military-grade rifle. Not only was he a lawyer who owned a law firm, but he also had a beautiful home in Town 'n' Country with ample backyard space and a basketball court. His wife, Jessica, was a midwife. They drove the latest car models, like Jaguars and Cadillacs, and switched them out every so often. His children, Shabazz and Genesis, even attended private school!

These things may sound ordinary or unexciting, but they left me in the purest state of culture shock. Here was a Black man who had achieved the American Dream, which I thought was reserved for White people and Latinos who were experts at assimilating. I loved Omar's life, every piece of it.

My favorite part of Omar's life is, beyond a shadow of a doubt, his personality. In all the years I've known him, I have never, ever heard Omar code-switch. What is that? Code-switching is when a person of color, most often a Black individual, changes their vernacular, dress, or mannerisms to blend in with their White counterparts. No matter what, Omar was a Black man from the South Side of Chicago. Nothing would ever change that.

He spoke freely, using every type of vernacular at his disposal: slang, college-level terminology, and everything in between. Outside of work, he wore comfortable athletic clothes with some Nikes or Jordans.

He also wasn't afraid to scold his children in public, a staple in Black and Brown communities. I witnessed Omar reprimand Shabazz on the baseball field with no concern for those watching.

Meeting Omar changed my understanding of the American Dream; it was within my reach, and I wouldn't have to stop speaking Spanish, marry a White man, or pretend to love Fall Out Boy to achieve it.

CHAPTER 20

Black Success

We were on the third or fourth family photo album, and she was still flipping through countless photos. By this point, we had traveled in time from Sheopatra's baby pictures to her high school dance-team memories, and all the heartwarming moments in between.

Now, we were jumping further back in time, before Sheo and her older brother, Charles, were born. This particular album brought us to the seventies and eighties. Sheopatra described each picture with the utmost detail. She recalled the names of every aunt, family friend, and church member.

"This is my momma. You see her next to him? That's my aunt Neidra who we visited yesterday. That woman looking overly fly? That's my granny, Beverly Streeter. I miss her every day. That's my girl."

We'd only been in Memphis for a few days, but I'd already fallen head over heels in love with the city. I adored it. Everyone was nice, and customer service employees were helpful and attentive. Phrases like "please," "excuse me," and "thank you" were part of everyone's vocabulary. I loved the people's accents. The Black-American country twang differed from the drawl of the sweet southern belle. Inevitably, Black people in Memphis inflected with an extra sauce. Compared to Los Angeles city life, it was like night and day.

Most people cared much more about manners. One afternoon, with eager bellies and take-out food in hand, we were leaving a local restaurant called Ching's Hot Wings. In front of us, a small family was also exiting. The mom and grandma passed through the front door first. As the little boy was leaving behind them, he glanced back at us, spun around, and stood up against the door, propping it open with his tiny body.

My heart just about exploded. He was holding the door for us! How adorable! With a big smile, I thanked the young gentleman as we passed him. I assumed that little boys like him were few and far between.

Young boys and men have held doors open for me in Tampa, but it's not commonplace. I would go out of my way to hold the door for an elderly person, but that was about it; the universe seldom returned the favor. When I was little, I overheard Papi tell his friend, "I hold doors open for women to watch them walk in." A sly smirk spread across his face before laughter ruptured their insides. I couldn't help but wonder if he ever held doors open to be polite, instead of in hopes of obtaining a free showing of the gluteus maximus.

In Los Angeles, or at least in the neighborhood I moved to, holding the door and even the most basic manners were practically nonexistent. By the end of our stay in Memphis, I had walked through numerous doors propped open not only by young boys and men, but by girls, women, and grandmas! Everyone I had the pleasure of running into was good-mannered. I fell in love!

While I was there, I only encountered White and Black people. Before my first trip, I'd heard Sheopatra talk about the racial demographic in Memphis many times, and her experience was 100 percent Black. The teachers, grocery store employees, doctors—everyone was Black. Of course, there were a few Mexicans, East Africans, and Asians. But the demographic during her upbringing was Blackity Black *Black*.

Back in the day, Whitehaven, the neighborhood Sheopatra grew up in, was a recent development with no Black people. In fact, Sheopatra's great-aunt, Cherry Streeter, was among the first group of Black people to purchase homes in the area. Like most stories of Black integration into White neighborhoods, they were met with intimidation and outright racism.

Fast-forwarding to decades later, Memphians nicknamed the locality "Blackhaven." There were no populations of White people in sight, unless you traveled further out to Germantown or Cordova, and even their demographics have shifted since our last few trips. The downtown area includes a mix of the two races. Still, with ongoing gentrification, Sheopatra has observed shifts in that demographic as well.

"When I was growing up, I never thought much of the White and Black neighborhoods," Sheopatra said. "What sparked my attention was how beautiful things in their neighborhoods were. Their McDonald's was either brand new or freshly renovated. The grocery stores were squeaky clean. And while driving through the streets, my behind wasn't bouncing up and down from unleveled streets. Early on, I noticed these White neighborhoods were tended to more often. *That's* what I minded.

I had no issue with the unofficial segregation. As a young Black girl, it was wonderful seeing an abundance of Black professionals. From a young age, I knew I could become anything I wanted. I saw examples everywhere. That's necessary for Black children."

Sheopatra Streeter comes from a long line of Black professionals. Her family earned college degrees during a time when many colleges didn't accept Black students. A great deal of their children also became college educated. Many of the Streeters sought professional careers in the school system, from teachers to guidance counselors. There are also psychiatrists, accountants, and engineers in the mix.

Meeting Sheo's family and learning about their circumstances caused me to reflect deeply. There I was, sitting in her mother's home, which had been Aunt Cherry's, with my eyes glazed over in awe. Her family's homes have roots planted in history. My family owns properties, too, but our roots remain on the island. Mita and Mami's house was the first seed planted in the US. It seemed as if most of She's family had achieved the American Dream. They were successful. When I tried to think of successful Black people from my upbringing, my mind went blank.

Back then, I had a different idea of success, and the only Black person I considered successful was Omar. I often wondered if he was the only successful Black person I knew as a kid. Some of my Black friends in school seemed to come from well-off homes, but I didn't know for certain. Most of our relationships didn't continue outside school hours. My close friend Chazz Cooks grew up in a large, beautiful home in Carrollwood, a wealthier neighborhood in Tampa. His mother, Tuty, one of my favorite humans, was single with three sons yet managed to keep everything together. That was quite impressive to me. His father, Alex Cooks, may he rest in peace, owned a bicycle store. Growing up, I couldn't name too many people with their own businesses, so Alex Cooks made a lasting impression on me.

Joia-Jordan Simone Johnson was another close friend from Orange Grove Middle School. We lost touch after attending different high schools, but we've stayed connected through social media. Although she was one of my good friends, I never saw Joia's house because we didn't make it to the sleepover stage. I didn't know whether her family passed my made-up test, but deep down, something told me Joia came from a pleasant home. She was intelligent. She always strived for greatness and had exceptional grades. Her outfits were crisp, clean, and put together, and her hair was always perfect. There had to be a caring momma behind the scenes, stressing the importance of looking presentable in public.

While writing this book, I reached out to Joia. As it turns out, her parents are college educated. Her momma had a few careers and owned a salon at one point. Her father, Larry Doby Johnson, was a professional baseball player. After being drafted straight out of high school, he played with the Indians, the White Sox, and the Tigers. After college, he obtained a master's degree and went on to become a teacher at two high schools, King and Middleton.

Learning about Joia's background confirmed every one of my teenage hypotheses. She was raised in a successful Black home.

It's difficult to measure the amount of successful Black people I knew because what in the world is success?! I soon realized there is no concrete answer to this; everyone has a different idea of prosperity.

For example, back then, I assumed home functionality was indicative of success. Did the hot water work? Did the doors open the way they should? Did anything require a delicate hand, a screwdriver, or a secret trick to operate? If not, looks like you're successful! I also based my perception of success on luxuries my family didn't have; pools, nice cars, and basketball courts in the backyard were all indicators.

After I turned eighteen and ventured into the adult world, my idea of success shifted. Everything in my apartment worked as it should. If there was an issue, the rental company or landlord handled it. Rent prices in Los Angeles were steep, and my apartment was the size of a shoebox, but by the grace of God, I was able to pay rent by the first of every month. My car note and insurance payment were more than what Mami paid for her car, Roberto's car, and their insurance combined, yet somehow I made ends meet. At that age, you couldn't tell me nothing! I was living on the opposite side of the country and paying my bills with no help from my mom. I swore up and down that I was successful. I had made it!

Nowadays, I still consider my earlier definition of success accurate. Life is tough! Being able to pay bills each month is something to celebrate. However, I've added layers to my personal definition of accomplishment.

In addition to paying bills, I'd also like to be able to take regular vacations. I'd like to set aside relaxation time at least every three months in a local resort or on an island in the Caribbean. Wherever I am, I don't want to worry about my bank account at all. I'd like to have children whenever I please. I don't want to continue holding off because I'm not as financially stable as I would like to be. Lastly, I want investments, assets, passive income, generational wealth, and the eradication of generational curses. And I want to achieve all these things with happiness, love, and healthy relationships with those around me. That is my definition of success in this stage of life. Someone down the street might define success as being a millionaire with a private jet or paying off a student loan, so the concrete definition is up to interpretation.

I've also recognized other kinds of success that I'd been around for my entire life. Immigrating to another country is triumphant. It's not easy to uproot yourself and plant new seeds in a country where you don't know the language. It's not easy to receive snide remarks from Americans when they hear the twang in your accent.

Mami was forced to move here as a teen and adapt to a new way of life. Mita went from being a stay-at-home parent in Puerto Rico to working two full-time jobs to keep the bills paid in Tampa. Roberto fled Cuba, leaving his son and family behind. His son spent years without a father while he followed hopes for a better life in the States.

Upon arrival, Roberto used every bit of talent he had to secure income and build his home life. In due course, he was able to move his son to Tampa. Papi always had multiple streams of income and businesses. He was the first person to introduce me to the concept of rental income. Back then, I couldn't fathom why anyone would purchase a home but live elsewhere! Before Omar, Chazz, Joia, or the Streeter family, Papi and Roberto were my first real examples of Black success.

CHAPTER 21

A Double Life

By the time I was in middle school, I considered myself a professional in social settings. Most of my White and kind-of-White Latino friends were at the dance studio. Most of my Black and "fresh off the boat" Latino friends were at school. Somehow, I learned to gracefully ping-pong between two different lives: a Black school life and a White dance-studio life.

In school, we cursed a lot. While adults weren't listening, profanities rained down. We dropped "shits" and f-bombs like our lives depended on it. Infamous Florida slang like janga, jit, and bih flew from our mouths often. My female friends and I called each other bitches and hoes, but in jest. It was about hyping each other up, like "Bitchhh, I love these new shoes you got on! Them cute! Where'd you get them from, ho?"

It was usually out of love, and we were quick to get on a girl if she used the words with a little too much attitude.

Like most teenage girls, we were boy crazy. My first girl crush was budding, but I still found boys attractive and didn't skip a beat during conversations about the finest boys in school. We passionately pit Lil' Romeo against Bow Wow: Who was the most good-looking? Who was fly? Which teenage heartthrob had the best dance moves? I expressed my preference for boys with dreadlocks, while a friend said a boy with a nice fade could take her number any day.

As far as hair, style, and features went, we had varying tastes. But the race of our boy crushes remained the same: Black, Black, bliggity *Black*. Daddy Yankee was a contender a couple of times, but for the most part, our type was all shades of beautiful brown skin.

We treasured music. Every time Tampa artists like Tom G, Strizzo, or Tae Bae Bae dropped a new song, we reported the news to each other the next day at school. The songs were wildly inappropriate, but we didn't care. In our makeshift girl-group formation, we sang "Clean Azz Pussy" by Tom G, like we were in the music video.

When I listen to these songs as an adult, I feel a mixture of nostalgia and embarrassment. On one hand, they remind me of some of the most fun times in my adolescence. On the other, I cringe thinking about a thirteen-year-old singing "Tongue Song" by Trina. Life changes when you become an adult. You evaluate all the stupid decisions from years ago. And boy, did I make some ill-advised and downright dangerous choices.

As soon as summer vacation hit, all the foolishness was on and poppin'. My close friends, cousins, and I spent all day talking to boys on Myspace. One of my cousins was about two years older and already in high school, so my fast behind chatted with her male friends, too. I exchanged numbers, flirted, and even put a few in my Top 8 on

Myspace, which at the time signified the utmost status on someone's friend list.

The only thing that stopped me dead in my tracks was one infamous question: "Do you have an older sister named Windaly?" Tire screech. Record scratch. Abort mission.

Windaly was also in high school, so it was common for my cousin and her to have mutual friends. Tampa was so small, and having a face nearly identical to my sister's didn't help. If this boy knew Windaly, he'd relay our conversation to her, and she'd deliver my rear end back to me on a platter.

If the boys didn't know my sister, I met up with them at theme parks like Busch Gardens, the mall, neighborhood parks, and teen nights—oh, the teen nights. Those were club-like events for ages thirteen to seventeen. That was only the suggested age range, and there was no system in place to enforce those restrictions, so a twelve-year-old Yorelis attended a few. The lack of enforcement allowed older folks to slip into these events as well.

I met quite a few older boys at teen nights. We'd spend most of the night dancing and flirting until I asked *the* question: "How old are you?" My neck snatched back every time I heard eighteen, nineteen, or twenty. One time, I even met a twenty-one-year-old!

Half of me thought it was weird. Why would they attend a club event for teens? They were old enough to get into an actual club! Mami said the teen club was expensive and that they were psycho to charge kids a twenty-five-dollar entry fee. If the adult clubs were cheaper, why was he here? However, these older guys showing interest intrigued the other half of me—the fast, no-good side. It was pretty cool meeting a guy who was already driving, had a car, and sometimes had an apartment. That side of teen Yorelis thrived off dumb kid logic and was blind to the predatory red flags these men were waving.

Nevertheless, the teen club was where it was at. It was the best place to holla and get holla'd at. Unfortunately, it was also the best place for lots of mess. There were *always* fights at the teen club. Shoot-outs and stabbings, too. They were always getting shut down. Fights broke out so often, my friends and I would make detailed plans of what to do, where to meet, and who to call.

I remember posting a status on Myspace that read, "Going to teen night at Skate World tonight. Do me a favor. If y'all tryna fight, please do that shit after eleven. I'm tryna get my money's worth, and y'all ain't about to mess that up!" The teen nights were from 9 p.m. to midnight, so I wasn't about to waste twenty-five dollars because there was a fight at 9:30 p.m.

Life was crazy with my Black friends. We swore we were grown, lived fast, and did some dangerous things, but hell, it sure was fun. I had fun at my White dance studio, too, but in different ways.

My White friends had no clue who any of the popular Black Tampa artists were. If I wanted to listen to any of that, I had to wait to see my Black friends at school. That didn't bum me out, though. It prompted me to pay attention to what my dance friends were listening to. They introduced me to many artists. Instead of rapping Lil' Kim lyrics word for word, we belted Taylor Swift, Fall Out Boy, and Panic! at the Disco.

Their music was generally clean, but my White friends cursed in everyday conversation, though the curse words were different. Instead of calling a girl a ho, she was a whore or a slut. They didn't use "ho" or "bitch" in friendly conversation. If they called someone a whore or a bitch, they meant it.

In Black life, at least during my adolescence, the most offensive thing you could do to someone was talk about their momma. Of course, there were "yo momma" jokes, like "yo momma's so fat, she got her own zip code." But if you went after someone's momma for real, you could expect voices to raise and fists to fly. The second-worst act was probably messing with someone's younger sibling.

In White life, the most treacherous thing was to call someone a cunt. Before hanging out with my White friends, I'd never heard the c-word. I laughed the first time I heard it and asked, "What the hell does that mean?" But I quickly learned the severity of the insult. I never added it to my Rolodex of curse words, but if my friends were called that or called another girl that, I'd clutch my pearls in shock.

A lot of my White friends had Facebook. At first, the idea of being on Facebook perplexed me. Why would we make a profile on a website created for college students? (To my young readers out there, Facebook was originally a platform for college students to connect.) A few of them had Myspace profiles, but they didn't use them often. Facebook was the place to be. Once I looked past the whole college thing, I ended up creating a Facebook profile. That was the beginning of my social-media double life.

In Myspace pictures, we posed with middle fingers up, peace signs leaning to the side, or hand symbols representing our neighborhoods. TC, West Tampa, Port of Tampa (pronounced with a country twang as *Poat* Tampa), and others had hand gestures and symbols to represent them. You already know what this Town 'n' Country girl was tossing up. (Fun fact: I didn't stop throwing up the TC sign in pictures until I moved to LA and noticed how similar it looked to the Crips symbol. I was not about to have people thinking I was a Crip.)

In Facebook pictures, my friends and I used vertical peace signs with the palms of our hands facing the camera. As a group, we did a "sorority pose" where we stood in two rows, and the front line would put their feet together and bend forward with their hands on their knees. They posted emo captions and pictures whenever they felt sad, or they put inspirational quotes in their image captions. I was accustomed to choosing the hottest Lil Wayne lyric.

I enjoyed hanging out with those friends, but we weren't booty-shaking the night away at a teen club. We went to their pools, rode their boats, hung out at their beach houses, and went to the mall. They shopped at stores like Hollister and Tory Burch. Many of my friends either had Tory Burch sandals or were begging their moms for a pair. Naturally, I asked Mami if she could buy me a pair, too. She didn't know what the brand was, but she said yes. However, as soon as she saw the price tag, we headed straight for the exit. In one swift motion, she yanked my head out of the clouds and reminded me I wasn't my dance friends. She said she didn't understand why people wasted money on flat *pedazos de mierda*, pieces of shit, anyway. Now that I've matured, I appreciate that. Because of her, I don't marvel at luxury purses or clothes. If a purse costs more than eighty dollars, I create a list in my head of the hundreds of ways I could spend those funds. The only things I drop money on without blinking an eye are food, my family, and my wife.

Besides the fatal price tags on their clothes, I didn't get into hazardous situations with my White friends. They didn't live in the projects. They didn't meet older guys, at least not with me. None of them attended teen nights, so they didn't experience shoot-outs or stabbings. Their dangers were different.

I had a friend named Sally who always drove too fast, ten-to-fifteen miles above the speed limit. She sped through neighborhoods, put on mascara at the wheel, and only paused for milliseconds at stop signs. I couldn't compare her driving to any of my Black friends since most of them didn't have cars. All I knew was that my armpits perspired every time I got into a car with her.

Sally was also notorious for taking oxycodone. I had no clue what kind of drug oxy was or where she purchased it, but she'd act nutty whenever she took it. Her speech slurred into long, drawn-out sentences, and a permanent smile stretched across her face. Although I didn't know what it was or what it was doing to her, I noted how often Sally took oxycodone—it was a lot.

During a sleepover in my junior year, we all went night-swimming in my friend's pool. We'll call this friend Becky. She lived in a beautiful house in a White neighborhood in Tampa that had a pool, a hot tub, and even a river. A couple of feet away from the pool, a long wooden dock extended to the river behind her house. There was also a boat moored at the dock.

That night, Becky had scored some alcohol out of her parent's liquor cabinet. She said they wouldn't notice it because there were hundreds of bottles. Come to find out, the liquor cabinet was actually a six-foot-long walk-in closet. It was a small liquor store!

I didn't drink with my Black friends, and if we did, it wasn't fancy liquor. All we could get our hands on was cheap malt liquor like Four Loko. None of our parents had a stocked liquor cabinet. Mami and Roberto might have had one or two bottles of rum in the fridge, but that was about it. Whether it was with us or on her own, it seemed like Becky was always drinking her parents' alcohol.

So there we were, passing around a water bottle full of Grey Goose vodka. We'd been drinking and flip-flopping between the pool and the hot tub for about an hour. I'm not sure whose bright idea it was, but someone suggested that we all jump in the river. The group of girls hummed with excitement. Then someone added, "Let's skinny-dip!"

My limbs stiffened. They lost me at "river." What the hell? A river? At night? In *Florida*, where alligators live? What about the leeches and the fish? What about the lethal freshwater bacteria talked about on the news every two months? With the currents, and the alcohol in our system?!

Before my thoughts fully unraveled, all the girls had gotten up, peeled off their swimsuits, and cannonballed into the water. I stepped out of the pool, tiptoed to the end of the dock, and sat down with my legs crossed.

"Come on, jump in!" they yelled.

"Hell naw! Y'all are crazy!" I laughed.

They continued splashing around while I watched from the dock.

I had a friend in this life who I'll call Jessica. I was closer to her than the others. She understood me. First off, she was born and raised in Town 'n' Country. She came from a big family like me, and her parents were also immigrants. Spanish was the primary language spoken at home. Jessica understood the hustle and bustle of TC; her mother had an essential job, and her family bargain-shopped and bought off-brand cereals just like mine. Jessica lived the first-generation, working-class immigrant life, but she also had a taste of White life.

Her grandparents owned two businesses and did well. They bought a home in Land O' Lakes, a pleasant, developing city outside Tampa, and they drove nice Cadillac SUVs. Jessica spent a lot of time at her grandparents' house. She even had a bedroom there. Using either her grandparents' or aunt's address, she attended predominantly White schools for most of her K–12 education.

Jessica was a first-generation kid, but she sometimes fell into the Americanized Latino category I'd invented. She was somewhat fluent in Spanish, like me. We weren't like our Americanized White-Latino dance friends who didn't speak or understand Spanish. Like mine, her parents worked hard, but Jessica could still enjoy the finer things in life with the help of her grandparents. She kept up with some of the name brands our White and White Latino friends wore. Her first car was a 2005 Kia, a beautiful first car in 2013 compared to my 1998 Honda.

At the end of each school day, I'd leave my Trick Daddy– and Marc Anthony–loving friends and unite with my Taylor Swift– and Selena Gomez–loving dance friends. Because Jessica attended White schools, dance studio life was no different for her. She always knew what artist or brand our dance mates were talking about. They also had similar taste in boys. Jessica liked handsome Spanish boys, but she had googly eyes for long-haired, blue-eyed White boys, too. White boys never caught my interest, except the finest—my fake husband Paul Walker, may he rest in peace.

Jessica bounced between White life and first-generation Latino life with little to no effort. We bonded through our Latino connection. She understood where I came from and my upbringing. When Jessica transferred to my high school for two years, she learned about my Black life, too.

By the end of that first year at Blake High School, Jessica had transformed. Once meek and timid, she now handled teenage drama with clapping hands and fighting words. Tampa slang started flowing from her mouth. At her former school, Jessica dealt with a bully for most of the year; now, she defended herself and no longer tolerated bullying. I was so proud to witness her thinning tolerance for mean girls as each day passed. Not only did Jessica learn about Tampa music artists, but she learned their songs word for word and sang them with me! She still preferred White and Latino boys, but she admitted a couple of Black boys at school were cute. Jessica even learned "Black people's rules."

I'm sure people of other races and ethnic backgrounds abide by these guidelines, but I was introduced to them by my Black friends. As an adult, I've noticed that most of my Black friends also follow this rubric almost instinctively, no matter where they grew up. Here are a few Black people's rules:

Bend your knees or drop to the floor when you hear something that sounds like gunshots, fireworks included.

Keep the exit in your line of sight while sitting in public

places. Don't sit with your back to the door. You don't know who's coming in or out.

Run away from fights, especially at a teen night. You never know if the fight will escalate into a shooting. It's best to run in the opposite direction as soon as the fight breaks out.

According to my teen logic, Jessica was finally learning street smarts. This was uplifting because a couple of years ago, a circumstance with Jessica forced me to think twice about her. It was summer vacation. I was still in middle school, and I believe Jessica was already in high school. This took place before she transferred. After getting dressed in our best attire, free from the restrictions of school dress codes, we were on our way to teen night. The plan was for my mom to drop us off and her mom to pick us up, a decision Jessica would later regret.

She started the night rather timidly. It was the first teen night she had ever attended. There were cute boys, and girls showing their middriffs in tank tops and booty shorts. Not only were these girls showing skin, but they were also professional dancers. I'm not talking ballerinas or modern dancers; I'm talking full-out, back-breaking booty shakers. They danced on guys for full songs, winding their hips in a thousand rotations.

I wasn't too sure, but judging from her anxiety, it seemed like Jessica had never danced on a guy before. At first, we danced side by side. I gyrated my rear end in a circle and watched as she repeated. I bounced my butt up and down to the beat and made sure she moved to the same sounds. One by one, her nerves melted away. In no time, she was throwing her butt left, right, up, down, and in circles. She was throwing it so well, a boy slid behind her from almost out of nowhere. He held her right hand while his left rested on her hip. She stiffened up a bit, and her eyes met mine. I widened my eyes and signaled my approval for the boy. In some telepathic, teenage-witch way, I was saying, "Do it, girl. He's cute! Throw it on 'em!" Jessica took a breath, bent her knees, and let the sounds of Tampa Tony guide her.

A silent scream ran through my head. My friend was out here at a teen night! She was outside of her White school and in a predominantly Black and Brown teen night, throwing it back! I was stoked.

As the night went on, Jessica grew more comfortable. We danced with boys and cranked that Soulja Boy together. Then, on the other side of the dance floor, two male voices rose, yelling phrases back and forth that we couldn't make out over the loud music. One thing was for sure, though: their voices did not sound friendly. As their dialogue continued, the volume of their voices increased. In the blink of an eye, a small circle had formed around the two boys, and fists were flying.

At first, I stood still next to Jessica and watched the situation across the room. But as soon as I saw a circle of bystanders, I grabbed Jessica's hand and took two steps toward the exit.

"Wait! What's going on?" Jessica shrieked.

"A fight, Jessica! We gotta go right—!"

Before I could finish my sentence, she had already released my hand and was running full speed toward the fight.

"What?!" I hollered.

I lunged after Jessica, fishing for her hand while weaving

through the crowd. When I caught up to her, the circle of kids had dissipated, revealing front-row seats to the scene. The only problem was that we arrived at the worst part of the show. As the kids dispersed, police shined their flashlights on the floor, where a boy clutching his stomach was sitting in a bright-red pool of blood.

"He got stabbed! He got stabbed!" teens yelled as they scurried away.

The house lights turned on. Now I could see the police officer holding a flashlight in one hand and a gun in the other.

"Everyone back up! Back the fuck up! Right now!"

He turned in a circle, pointing his weapon at all the teenage onlookers. Jessica and I were about ten feet away. I grabbed Jessica's hand and, with all my force, sprinted to the exit. We hit a bit of traffic, but the bulk of the escaping stampede subsided. About thirty teens were shuffling out of the door. While Jessica and I waited to be picked up, the scene outside intensified. First, there was one police car. Then another pulled up. Shortly after, an SUV-sized cruiser arrived. Five minutes later, several police cars riddled the parking lot. Even an ambulance was there to pick up the boy who had been clutching his bleeding stomach.

When Jessica's mom showed up, she was furious. She chewed Jessica out the entire ride home, forbidding her from ever attending another teen night. I was upset with her, too. Who the hell runs toward a fight? The way people be shootin' for any petty reason, who in their right mind would run toward an altercation?! That was the Whitest thing I've ever seen Jessica do.

As I paced back and forth in my bedroom that night, I

was in disbelief. I thought she could join me for a teen night and experience my Black life for a bit, the life I lived at school. But she couldn't go anywhere with me if she was going to continue that idiocy! What if the fight had turned into a shooting? What if stray bullets sprayed the circle where we had front-row seats? Why didn't she know what to do if a fight broke out? We'd been living different lives.

A few years later, when Jessica transferred to my high school, she learned her Black people rules. But two years don't wipe out all those previous years in White schools. That's why I ended up sitting on a dock alone that night while Jessica and our friends frolicked in the river. The closest friend I had in that world was still a product of her surroundings, which were predominantly White. In addition to some liquid courage, that's what led her to jump into a river without an inkling of what could go wrong.

After moving to LA, my perspective broadened. I learned that running toward a fight and feeling free enough to jump into an alligator-infested river aren't solely White things. LA introduced me to a plethora of Black, carefree folk who reminded me of my childhood White friends.

Sometimes, my Black and White worlds mixed. It was inevitable. It's impossible to lead a double life without some leakage. At times, brutal slang and Ebonics slipped from my mouth in the White world. I was probably just talking too fast to code-switch. I'd notice the leakage because one of my friends would repeat a word or phrase back.

"Gon'?" I heard a girl echo under her breath one day. She noticed it sounded different from "going to" or "gonna."

The worlds could blend in hilarious ways, like me telling

my White friend she had a "fat cat." A woman has a fat cat if she has large labia. For some reason, young boys liked that and talked about it often. So, as a good friend, I felt it was my duty to let her know. She giggled and brought it up for the next few days at dance. Her boyfriend liked it, and she noticed her mom had one as well.

However, now and then, the worlds didn't mix too well, like the day I told a girl in the White world that her butt looked big. I was taken aback when tears emerged from the corners of her eyes. What? I thought. It's a compliment! Her butt looked big in those jeans she wore that day. Why was she upset?

In the Black world, my friends and I constantly talked about how much we wanted big butts. We tracked the growth of our butts, whether it was real or not. "Girl, I swear my booty gettin' bigger," we'd announce to each other. But big butts weren't a good thing in the White world, at least not back then. Nowadays, there's a heavy influx of White women doing squats and getting butt procedures done. I guess things change.

When I was twenty-two, I had the opportunity to go on a big tour with a White pop artist. We'll call her Ms. Bubblegum. My White friends had introduced me to the artist years prior. I hadn't listened to her music since, but that was nothing a little research couldn't fix. Come to find out, Ms. Bubblegum never stopped producing hits!

Her tour had the works: props, a massive stage, thousands of synchronized lights, and the biggest show of them all—fireworks. Every night, in the middle of the last song, fireworks burst into the sky from different parts of the venue. She literally closed her shows with a bang. We used them for the entire six-month tour, and it took me a while to memorize the sequence in which they would shoot. At the end of the show, after the "thank you"s and bows, the final firework would explode. By the time it illuminated the sky, we'd be backstage, or at least halfway there.

After finishing up a show in a city I can't remember, everyone was on their way backstage. Makeup running, breathing heavily, and energy buzzing, we celebrated another appearance checked off the list. Some dancers, including me, and some members of the band walked in front of Ms. Bubblegum. The others traveled behind. Big smiles stretched across our faces while we congratulated each other on another completed show. We eagerly looked forward to the food and wine that awaited us at the hotel.

Just then, a *boom* rattled the stadium, startling all of us. Most people raised their eyebrows or bent their knees ever so slightly. Not me—in one swift movement, I dropped to the floor and laid as flat as a pancake, my knees and elbows pressed against the floor like I was doing an army crawl. As the lights brightened the air, everything became clear: it was just a firework.

Before getting up, I glanced at Ms. Bubblegum a few inches behind me. Her eyes went wide before a hearty chuckle of amusement and shock escaped her mouth.

I laughed awkwardly. "My bad. I thought it was something else."

Within one moment, everyone—Ms. Bubblegum, her mostly White team, the stage crew, and the band—could guess the type of upbringing I had. Why else would I assume the loud sound was a gunshot? If I was on the outside looking in, I'd guess I had a rough upbringing or that I was a war veteran.

I don't know if I'd consider that a "bad" example of my White and Black worlds mixing. I wasn't embarrassed, just taken aback. Maybe the rise in mass shootings contributed to my reaction. Unfortunately, mass shootings were becoming widespread in America at that time, and some of them occurred at concerts. Whatever the reason for my reaction, I guessed that most of these people probably weren't crawling out of teen clubs when they were in middle school.

CHAPTER 22

On Alert

O n two separate occasions, I heard non-Black friends say the N-word in casual conversation. And each time, I fell into silent waves of shock that prevented me from starting a dialogue or confronting them. I told myself I would never let that happen again.

As strange as it may sound, I now watch my non-Black friends closely. In the beginning, and even after years of friendship, I examine them and listen. My past friends let the bomb drop at least a year into our relationships, so I figured that it's best to remain on alert. I want to observe, see if they switch up or if they continue to respect my boundaries. I say *my* boundaries because some Black people don't care or even encourage non-Black people to say the word. Not me. They can drop all the N-words their heart desires around *those* friends, but they must use the power of common sense and remember that all Black people are not the same, just as all White people are not the same. Not every White person is a racist, gun-toting, hardcore Trump enthusiast, and it would be psychotic to treat every White person as if they were. So, if you have a Black friend who allows you to say the N-word, it would be psychotic to believe that every Black person agrees with this ideology. It would be outlandish to say, "But Jamal lets me use it," as if Jamal is the spokesperson for the entire race.

I don't set traps for my friends. I don't ask them to read aloud text messages where the word is used, I don't call them the N-word to perceive their reaction, and I most definitely don't ask them to sing specific songs to see if they'll say it. I just sit back and let the moments come naturally. While rapping lyrics, I'll say the word when it arrives while inconspicuously side-eyeing the friend beside me. If I'm in a group, I'll watch the mouths of all the non-Black people in the room, waiting to see what the outcome will be.

I'm not the only Black person who does this. During these moments, I've locked eyes with many brothers and sisters who have the same agenda. If someone utters the word in a public setting like that, the outcome isn't usually immediate confrontation. In my case, I'll make a mental note and file it in the back of my brain: "Remember, Susan is the type of person to sing the N-word without a care in the world. Remember that if you were ever to build a relationship with her." Friends and acquaintances aren't the only people subject to review. I've conducted the same silent investigations with bosses and choreographers in my line of work.

No one has said the N-word in front of me since my two friends did. But if the time comes, I'm prepared to make a simple and quick reply: "Hey, please don't say that around me. It makes me uncomfortable. I hope you can respect that." Nothing less and nothing more. If those words result in outrage from the other person, that further proves I'm not being heard. They don't respect me, nor do they care about my comfort.

CHAPTER 23

Fulana

Fulana *(feminine) or* Fulano *(masculine) is
another way of saying "what's-her-name"
or "what's-his-name."*

I t's synonymous with "that person" or "young
man/young lady." I'm not sure if it's solely Puerto
Rican slang. In my hometown, most Spanish speakers
use the word. Puerto Ricans, Cubans, and Dominicans live
in the same neighborhoods and rub shoulders, so we often
exchange vernacular. I've heard different Spanish-speaking
Caribbeans use it, but its origin remains a mystery. Perhaps
one of my readers can school me.

We often use Fulano when we don't know someone's
name, like the cashier at the supermarket.

"What happened to your eggs? They're all broken."

"I don't know. Fulano must've packed them at the
bottom of the bag."

Sometimes, we use Fulana in a vindictive manner. When I was younger, my cousin dated a girl whom most of my family was not a fan of. We exchanged some brief words with her, but she had a possessive, argumentative aura, not to mention that my cousin always seemed stressed out when he was with her. Because of our protective and slightly shady nature, no one ever said his girlfriend's name. We all knew her name and called her by it in her presence. But as soon as she left, her name no longer existed.

"Did you see how Fulana was controlling his every move?"

"Oye, Fulana threw away her plate full of food earlier. How wasteful."

I was too young to take part, but it was entertaining to watch the older family members nitpick.

Years ago, I was granted the opportunity to go on a national tour with a male R&B artist, who I'll call Mr. Smooth Daddy. I'm not sure if his good looks or suggestive lyrics were to blame, but women flocked to him left and right. In every city, ladies hunted down his tour bus and collected outside of the arena hours before the concert. Mr. Smooth Daddy didn't mind; he welcomed the attention with open arms.

During each concert, a few members of his entourage would scour the audience in search of beautiful women to bring backstage for his infamous dressing room after-party. There, music pounded from the speakers all night, and they supplied Hennessy by the boatloads. Whether I wanted to party or just sip on a beverage before crawling into my bunk, I rarely missed an after-party.

Some women gawked at Mr. Smooth Daddy from across

the room but never spoke to him. Others talked his ear to shreds. Some women tried to seduce him with drunken hip rolls and an unbalanced stance. I saw it all. I didn't know these women, so there was no rude intention or malice. I simply couldn't keep up with the conveyor belt of women from city to city, so Fulana was their name—*all* of their names.

"Did y'all see Fulana in the pink at the after-party last night? She wasted no time taking off her heels and twerking on the table!" I'd report to the other dancers.

"Omg. Y'all won't believe what happened. I'm packing up, getting ready to go to the bus for the night, and Fulana walked out of *our* dressing-room bathroom with my makeup bag in her hand!"

By the end of the tour, all the dancers had adopted the slang into their vocabulary.

"How was the after-party last night? I didn't go. Sleep hit me hard."

"Oh, it was good. The usual. Fulanas everywhere."

CHAPTER 24

The Token

O ne of my recent jobs was a twelve-hour music-video shoot filled with lots of hurry up and wait, a common phenomenon in the entertainment industry.

Hurry, get your hair and makeup done at 7 a.m.! Get dressed in the wardrobe and wait for the artist to arrive or for technical issues to be rectified—many hours later. Rush the talent to set like a herd of sheep and wait one additional hour for other unforeseen events. "Hurry up and wait" is the nature of the game, and by the grace of God, after six years in the industry, I'm finding ways to acclimate. Whether it's a joint, a good book, a nap, or several visits to the snack table, I've learned to pass the time without going mad.

On this set, we had trailers—not the old ones with the eighties carpet and an odor-filled couch, but new, beautifully decorated trailers. Four or five dancers occupied each trailer, but I didn't care. This treatment was outstanding compared to our normal circumstances. When I discovered a reputable taco truck parked in the lot that was at our disposal for the entirety of the shoot, I was in heaven. Our call time was 9 a.m., and I began the day with a sausage and bacon breakfast burrito. I'd been living a pescatarian lifestyle, but I deemed this shoot as a day of splurging.

Holding a burrito the size of an AriZona Tea can, I planted myself on the couch in the trailer. We discussed the usual morning topics: fatigue, LA traffic, caffeine withdrawals, deliriousness.

"We need Fulana One, Yoe, and Fulana Two in makeup right now," the choreographer yelled into the trailer, just as the savory bacon was meeting my taste buds.

"Got you," I said, setting my burrito down. This is the glamorous life, right?

I plopped into the makeup chair as the artist pulled multiple brown shades out of her kit. Before applying the eyeshadow, she rubbed a thick layer of primer on my skin.

"This waterfall scene is about to be wet!" she joked. "We gotta make sure this makeup is set by the gods!"

"Wait, what waterfall scene?" I asked. "I thought we were doing a rain scene."

"Yes, there is a rain scene, but that's later tonight. The waterfall scene's in a couple of hours."

I'd usually have a better idea of which scenes I was a part of, but to be honest, details from our long rehearsals got blurred in my memory. We workshopped a lot, tried a lot of different ideas, added to and subtracted from the choreography. By the end of the nine-hour rehearsal the night before, I wasn't sure what section I was in, which routines made the cut, or the names of the scenes I was a part of.

"You aren't in the waterfall scene," another dancer called from across the room.

After double-checking with the choreographer, we solved the mystery: I wasn't in the waterfall scene and didn't have to be in makeup. I rose from the chair and another dancer took my place. If the scene didn't shoot for a couple of hours, and the dancers just started hair and makeup, that meant a two-to-three-hour nap was my fate.

Envisioning a wholesome slumber, I practically jogged back to the trailer. When I arrived, the only other person present was Leah, a female dancer I'd never worked with before. Then again, there were quite a few women on the job I didn't know. Los Angeles is an enormous city, but the dance industry can feel microscopic. While the community's small, it's easy to lose track of who's who with a conveyor belt of new dancers rolling in every year. I only spent a little time with her, but Leah was nice.

"Are you in the waterfall scene?" I asked.

"Nope."

"Girl, me either. But they sent me to makeup by accident."

I was glad to be reuniting with the juicy burrito I'd left behind.

For the next hour and a half, Leah and I talked about everything under the sun: our love lives, past jobs, hometowns, and most topics beyond basic small talk.

Knock knock! "Make sure you ladies have a base on! Makeup is running behind, so we're trying to make things as efficient as possible," the choreographer called from outside the trailer.

A mixture of terror and shock overtook me. I consider my makeup skills to be underneath the below-average line. With a little foundation, eyeliner, and lipstick, I can throw something together to get on stage, but that's as far as my expertise goes. In an arena or stadium, fans are so far from us that they can't spot errors, so I'm free to be mediocre. Cameras, however, capture a crystal-clear, high-definition picture that highlights every discrepancy.

"I have some foundation if you need it. I have bronzer, too," Leah offered. She must've read the absolute horror on my face.

"Thanks, boo, cause Lord knows I have nothing but BB cream." Relief swept over me. Leah was White, but her complexion had an olive tone to it, so our skin tones weren't that different.

As I clumsily slapped foundation onto every inch of my face, Leah opened up a little more. "One time, I did this job where the choreographer had hired me a day before the shoot. The girl I was replacing got booked on something else, so they put me in. Before they added me, the cast was all Black, so that's what the makeup team was prepared for. When I sat down in the chair, they were dumbfounded. They hadn't been told I was added, so they only brought different shades of brown. I also didn't have any of my makeup with me, so I walked around that set for the rest of the twelve-hour shoot three shades darker than my natural skin color. Weeks after that job, I still didn't post pictures. I didn't want people to think that was my choice."

My jaw gaped open. I was astounded, but also tickled. This was a familiar story, but I'd always heard it coming out of the mouths of Black women. I wouldn't be honest if I said I didn't find humor in the irony of Leah's story. She took no offense to the giggles that escaped my mouth.

"Girl! What?!" I laughed.

She chuckled, too. "I have no clue! All I know is my face looked like a brown pancake on a white popsicle stick all day!"

We hollered.

"I'm so sorry, love. Shoot, I'm glad you can laugh about it now, but I know it must've felt crazy. I hate when the hair or makeup department drops the ball."

"It's okay. To be honest, situations like that have been happening to me more often. I've been doing a lot of jobs where I'm the token White girl. If it's not makeup, it's the hair department. I'm not mad, though. I guess I'm just blown away. These are stories you usually hear from Black women. It's crazy to be in their shoes. This *just* started happening to me. I can't believe it's like that for them most of the time."

CHAPTER 25

Big Butt

We grabbed our packed lunches and traveled to dance studio 3, our regular lunch spot. After that grueling two-hour ballet class, our appetites were through the roof.

Chomping away, we talked, gossiped, and discussed important matters in our teenage lives. I'd always been younger than the others. While most of my dance friends recounted stories from their high schools, I did so with Orange Grove Middle School as my backdrop. The hour-long break passed in the blink of an eye, and before we knew it, it was time to clean up and get ready for yet another ballet class.

It was ballet week during summer dance camp, and I was surviving five hours of ballet every day, Monday through Friday: barre, across the floor, classical variations, contemporary ballet, and pointe work. The rigorous hours were crucial for my training; it made me an overall better dancer. My flexibility and stamina always improved after summer dance camp. It was the perfect reintroduction to the fall season.

But if heard a single classical piano key on the weekend, I'd lose it.

With wrappers and empty sandwich bags in hand, we made our way toward the trash bin at the other end of the studio. I caught a glimpse of Emily in front of me. She always had the best leotards; this one zipped in the front, and black lace sprawled over her back. It had to be expensive. I knew this because I'd made it a personal quest to research the cost of one of her leotards so that I could ask my mom for the same. My search came to a screeching halt once I read seventy-five dollars. My mother didn't spend more than thirty dollars on my leotards, and that was pushing the limit. After that day, I knew I'd only admire Emily's leotards from afar.

My eyes followed the black lace. It swirled around, forming the shapes of flowers and then transitioning back into individual swirls. The lace began at the top of her shoulders and extended all the way to her—*Damn!* Her butt! I couldn't help but notice her rear end. It protruded from the sides of her hips and formed a full, perky bubble. When did her butt get big and how? The answer to my questions revolved around the wonders of puberty. We were in that age group, and our hormonal, adolescent bodies were changing every day. However, I assumed there was some methodical plan that explained Emily's growth. I needed to know her secrets.

"Emily! Your butt looks so big! What are you doing? Is it bread? My aunt says if you eat a lot of bread, it'll make your booty bigger. It hasn't worked for me, though."

"Uh, I don't know what I've been doing," she said softly. "It just started growing out of nowhere."

"Well, when you find out, let me know!" I replied.

After tossing the crust of my sandwich into the trash, I turned back toward the dance studio. I'd taken about three steps when I heard something—soft weeping. Sobs. I spun around to see Emily frozen at the trash can, her head hung low between her sunken shoulders that bounced up and down with her sobs.

I jogged back to her. "Emily, what's wrong?!"

"You ... said ... my butt ... was big."

I hadn't expected that to come out of her mouth. Despite my shock, laughter escaped my lips before I could stop it. "What? Big? Girl, that's not a bad thing! I pointed it out cause that's what I want! You gettin' thick, girl!"

"Thick?" Emily sniffled.

"Yes, thick! That means you got body! You got curves—tatas, butt, or both! And girl, you got the butt! Boys like that!" I grabbed her shoulders and looked directly into her eyes. By now, her sobs were transforming into soft sniffles, with one tear suspended on her cheek.

"They do?" Emily wiped the remaining tear away.

"Hell yeah! At least boys at my school do. They're always looking at the girls with big butts! Not at me, though, not with these flat cheeks!" My joke caused Emily to burst into laughter.

I apologized for my comment and reiterated that I didn't mean to hurt her feelings. I tried to explain further how much I wanted a body like hers, but Emily didn't want to hear any of it. She wanted to know more about boys liking big butts and why.

Now, I live in a world where the pencil-thin White European model is still in, but so is a voluptuous, plus-size

Black woman with an Afro, or a handsome man in a wheel-chair. Inclusivity is the wave. Companies realize it's in their best interest to market to everyone, instead of only to a small portion of society. I remember when the ballet world preferred ultra-lean, almost frail bodies. And I remember dancers like Misty Copeland breaking down those barriers with their gorgeous, muscular builds. Fast-forward to the present day, I'm watching White women get lip injections and butt implants to attain their idea of beauty.

One side of me has a lot of opinions on women molding their bodies to look more like Black women. It's baffling to witness them run toward the exact thing they once feared or even ridiculed. A part of me is livid that "thick" is becoming the new thing after watching women avoid it like the plague. The other half of me, however, doesn't care. I couldn't care less. I just hope naturally thick White girls like Emily aren't bursting into tears because of their rear ends. I don't know where Emily is today, but I hope she's out there sporting Daisy Dukes and flaunting that big butt right now.

CHAPTER 26

I'm Sorry

A ny journey of growth comes with discomfort. It has its difficulties, moments of victory accompanied by moments of uneasiness. Sometimes, it might feel like the path is nothing but uncomfortable.

As I was growing up, many adults, including those in my family, uttered many questionable statements about Black Americans and Black Latinos. They strived to meet European standards of beauty just as the people in most colonized countries did. They commented on the hair textures of my siblings and me, and they also drew comparisons between our complexions and those of our fathers—all features directly attributed to the Black DNA running through our veins. I revisited these memories in my adulthood, addressing what was offensive and inappropriate.

In retrospect, these moments affected me quite deeply. My family's actions caused me to look inward, hurling me into waves of self-realization and forcing me to evaluate my own actions. Maybe I had unknowingly affected others in the same way.

In elementary school, we formed lines to travel anywhere on the school grounds. Going to lunch? Get in line. Heading to the bus at the end of the day? Get in a straight, alphabetized line. One day in my fourth-grade class, the teacher, Mrs. Meyer, instructed us to line up. It was time to sprint outside for PE class.

"Let's try something different today," Mrs. Meyer began. "Let's line up in alphabetical order, but backwards! Letter Z in the front and letter A in the back."

"Whoa, what?" The students' energy buzzed throughout the room.

"You have one minute. Go!"

All at once, we raced to the front of classroom.

"K! P! T!" We yelled out the first letters of our last names, hoping to speed up the process.

Typically, I held the second position in line right behind Britney Allen or, as Mrs. Meyer called her, Ms. Allen. She preferred to address us by our last names; I guess it was about learning correct formalities. Because of this, my classmates and I were forced to learn each other's first names on our own, or use a classmate's last name as a nickname. We called Britney Allen "Allen." Terrance Thompson was just Thompson.

No one referred to me as Apolinario, though. Apple-Oreo was my name, or Ms. Apple-Oreo to Mrs. Meyer. She bestowed the nickname upon me on the first day of school when she declared my last name was too difficult to say. From that day on, I was Apple-Oreo.

Whether it was Apolinario or Apple-Oreo, the first two letters of my name remained the same. Second from the beginning transformed to second to last, and Allen would be the last in line. With about fifteen seconds left on the clock, I planted my feet in the back of the line.

"Ms. Allen," the teacher called out, "I believe you're in the A section of the line. You have the easiest position. You were first in the line, so now you're the end."

Allen snickered as she ambled to the back of the line. When I turned back, her snickers transferred over to me, causing us to burst into laughter.

"Quiet in the line, kids. I'm going to get my lunch out of the fridge, and then we can head out."

The fridge was in a smaller storage room that connected our classroom to Mr. Peterson's next door. It had a fridge, extra boards, and, according to legend, a secret stash of candy. While Mrs. Meyer retrieved her lunch, Allen and I continued to giggle uncontrollably. In an effort to compose myself, I whipped around with my arms behind my back, facing the front of the line. My giggles were now directed at the back of Keisha Black's head—or Ms. Black, according to Mrs. Meyer.

"What're you laughing at?" Black snarled.

Keisha Black dealt with a lot of behavioral issues. With her quick tongue and lethal attitude, she sassed teachers and classmates. She wasn't a bully; she just wasn't a nice girl. She rolled her eyes, and mean phrases raced rapid-fire from her mouth. I'd never encountered her wrath, but most of the class had experienced their own tense situations with Black —everyone except Clay.

Dayzha Clay was the only person I'd seen Black be nice to. From the first day of school, they clicked. Whenever Black was around Clay, her brow softened, her attitude subsided, and she even joked and smiled. Every other moment, she delivered "stank face" to the world, just like the stank face she shot me while I laughed behind her.

"I'm laughing at Allen. She's playing around." My giggles ceased.

"Yeah, that's what I thought, four eyes. Shut up," she said, turning toward the front of the line.

"Four eyes?!" My face contorted. "You shut up, Black burnt toast!"

Sporadic giggles erupted throughout the line. Her eyes darted back to me. She glared at my stank face behind the thick, crooked glasses on my nose. I glared back, scanning her seething expression, furrowed eyebrows, and her beautiful, dark-brown skin.

"All right, that's enough! Quiet in the line!" Mrs. Meyer emerged from the closet, ending the standoff between Black and me. She turned around to face the front of the line, and I released a long sigh. With one overall lame comeback, I had survived my first and only altercation with Keisha Black. She said little to me for the rest of the year.

Keisha, from the bottom of my heart, I am so sorry. We were bickering nine-year-olds, but that's no excuse. My comment was wild, inappropriate, and just plain mean. I went straight for the jugular. I'm especially upset that none of the children laughed when you called me four eyes, but they laughed when I made fun of your skin.

CHAPTER 27

A Black Man in America

I was sipping my beer and shaking my head in disbelief. A couple of yards away, RJ and Gerald, or Gerrie, were firing trash talk at each other as they jogged up and down the neighborhood basketball court. Their once baby fat–ridden bodies had transformed into lean, muscular builds. Facial hair had replaced the spaces where chubby cheeks used to be.

LA was my new home, but I kept up with RJ's tussle with puberty through FaceTime. Inches springing from his heels, pimples, the thick bass filling his voice, sprinkles of hair emerging on his chest—I was present for all of it, at least in a virtual sense. Gerrie, RJ's friend since childhood, went through his puberty journey away from my virtual gaze; instead of slowly processing his physical changes, I experienced them like dusk to dawn. A hyper, bright-eyed boy waved me off at the airport when I moved away. Then, three years later, a tall, too-cool-for-school teenager struggled to muster up a simple "hello." Gerrie was growing up. The little boy's absence saddened me a bit, but RJ had also morphed into a supercool teen, so I was used to it.

"Gerrie is so tall and handsome! He was at least three inches shorter last time I visited," I said to his father, Thomas.

"I know. I can't believe it," Thomas replied. "He's really growing up."

Reality had set in. They weren't boys anymore; they were young men—cute young men with high, moisturized Afros and fragments of swagger. That combination meant cute, young women weren't too far away. Oh, Lord. Girls...

"Gerrie must have the girls going crazy in school. I know RJ does. I'm trying not to be the psycho older sister." I laughed.

A hint of a smile stretched across Thomas's face, but it dissipated in a flash. "I need Gerrie to take a break from the girls for a while. He had me stressed out a few weeks ago."

"What happened?"

Thomas inhaled and exhaled. "Yoe, he's been dating this Cuban girl. Respectful and pretty young lady, blue eyes and long, blond hair. She's super nice, but her parents are a nightmare."

"What do you mean?"

"At the beginning of the month, her father interrupted our family dinner. He was banging on our front door. Banging like the police, with all his might."

In a mix of disbelief and disgust, my upper lip contracted upward. "What? Why the hell would he knock on your door like that?"

"To tell me that our kids shouldn't be dating. When I asked why, he rambled on. They are too young. They are cut from different cloths. Then..." His eyes studied the ground while he shook his head. "Yoe, he said they can't be together because his daughter is going places and my son isn't."

"What the %@*#?! Gerrie's the son of two doctors. Is he out of his mind?" Rage clouded my vision.

"It's been a while since I was forced to keep my composure that way. But I took a breath. I said, 'Sir, you drive the same car my sixteen-year-old son drives—the same Honda SUV. Both of his parents are doctors. What do you mean he isn't going places?' He went on with some other BS, trying to apologize and retract what he'd said. But it was too late. I knew exactly what he meant." Thomas sighed.

I finished the thought for him: "He meant his White Cuban daughter couldn't date a Black boy. He must be a future criminal, lowlife, or whatever stereotype he learned on TV."

"Exactly. You know, when I opened the door, I was ready for him to tell me an actual offense my son committed. Pictures, risky texts, or anything teens do these days. But when he kept saying vague things like 'they aren't cut from the same cloth,' I knew exactly what it was. I knew because I had dealt with it enough in my life.

I just thought my son wouldn't experience it until much later. But that time is here now. It snuck up on me. Gerrie's not a little boy anymore. He's a threat, a gangbanger, a criminal. He's a Black man in America."

CHAPTER 28

Pretty for a Black Girl

A lot of Latinos have fake aunts and uncles: close friends of our parents gifted the *Tia* or *Tio* title, or an elder cousin too old to be disrespectfully called by their first name.

Out of all my aunts, real or fake, Titi Paola is one of my favorites. Kindness doesn't begin to describe the warm, sugary, delicate cupcake that is her heart.

Outside of Mami, raw and unfiltered affection isn't a strong suit for many women in my family. Love was an ingredient Mita used in her cooking. We tasted it each time our grandma's phenomenal food skimmed our taste buds. We felt it every time she asked if we'd eaten, and every time she insisted we should eat anyway. But she never really said "I love you." A promising "Dios te bendiga," *God bless you*, was more her style.

Tia Mayra showcased her love with compliments and admiration.

"Ay, mi sobrina bella." *Oh, my beautiful niece.*

"Dios mio, que nena tan linda." *My God, what a pretty girl.*

Praise and compliments came often, but "I love you" was scarce.

But endless pools of love poured from Titi Paola. Bouts of silence were no match for her; she'd attack with hundreds of *besitos,* kisses, followed by multiple declarations of those three special words: *"Muah!* I love you! *Muah!* I! *Muah!* Love! *Muah!* You!" She'd kiss the side of my head until my hair frizzed.

Titi Paola lived in Puerto Rico, so I never spent a lot of time with her. But during every vacation to the island, it felt as though she had never left my side.

When I was twenty-two, I planned a vacation to Puerto Rico. No mom, no siblings—just Sheopatra and me. Mami had recently returned home from an unplanned month on the island. She arrived in Puerto Rico having only booked a one-way ticket. Then days turned into weeks, and a month had flown by before she purchased the return ticket. Her "quick trip" had become a month-long sabbatical. It would've been ludicrous to invite her back less than two months later, not to mention that Roberto would've missed her too much.

I pushed my nerves aside, strapped my vacation sandals in place, and called my Titi Paola. By this time, it had been eight years since my last trip to Puerto Rico. Outside of a birthday wish or a "Merry Christmas," I hadn't really kept up with Titi Paola. But the love she'd cultivated during my last visit to Puerto Rico was still fresh in my heart. There was no other option than to stay with her during our trip. It would be a beautiful opportunity to reconnect with my aunt.

The little fourteen-year-old she knew had grown up, and a young adult stood in her place: a professionally dancing, somewhat successful, *lesbian* adult. How would she react to her niece and her niece's girlfriend staying in her home? Would she even let us? She was in her late sixties, and she was also a devout Catholic. That combination rarely screams gay pride. What if she said no? My brain performed somersaults for the few days I spent calculating every potential worst outcome. Eventually I mustered up the courage to call Titi Paola.

"Hola, Titi."

"Hola, mi princesa. Cómo estás?"

"I'm good," I responded, switching to English. Titi Paola lived in Chicago for a few years, so her English is impeccable, almost better than Mami's at times. "Titi, do you remember the dates for my visit to Puerto Rico?"

"Yes, *mija*. I have the dates written on my calendar. Are you still coming to stay with me?"

"Of course. I just wanted to ask you... Is it okay if someone comes with me, and stays at your house with me?"

"*Si, mi amor.* Is a friend coming with you?"

"Um, no, Titi. My girlfriend is coming with me. I don't know if you know that about me. It's been a while since I've seen you. And it's okay if you don't want us to stay with you. I'd understand." In a single moment, I had regressed to the scared fifteen-year-old girl, terrified to reveal to her mother that the extravagant Valentine's gifts she received weren't from a boy.

Silence reigned for what felt like an eternity. I started

considering hotel options in Juana Díaz. How much would that cost? We'd set aside funds for the trip, but would that cover food, transportation, and a hotel room for seven days? I felt my wallet tighten in the back of my jeans. We would have to save more money if—

"Yorelis, of course you guys can stay with me," she said, interrupting my unraveling thoughts. "Both of you are welcome in this home."

"Really?" The tension evaporated from my shoulders.

"Claro," she reiterated. *Of course.* "And *mija*, I already knew about your situation. You told me that one time you and your mom visited Chicago when I still lived there. You cried in my lap. You were upset because of all the hurtful things your grandmother said to you. She didn't accept you."

In an instant, the memories flooded back: Mami and I touching down in Chicago for a dance convention, visiting my extended family, seeing Titi Paola for a moment—and my body curled up in a wide, marshmallow coat, hunched over on my aunt's lap, bawling my eyes out. The memory became crystal clear. I had just come out to my family not too long before that, and when Mita found out, she said things a grandmother should never say to her grandchild. After spending time with Titi Paola and once again feeling her unconditional love, I felt comfortable enough to reveal my troubles to her.

"Oh wow, Titi. I almost forgot about that. You know, before that moment, I never really told anyone how Mita's words made me feel, but it all came out around you. I couldn't control it."

"Well, you know, *mi amor*, I'll love you no matter what.

And I'm sorry your grandmother reacted like that. Life's too short to turn away family. I can't wait to meet your girl-friend. Where is she from?"

Waves of relief moved through my body. "I can't wait for you to meet her either. She's Black and from Tennessee, but she knows a little Spanish. She's a quick learner and can roll her *r*'s better than me!"

"De verdad?" Titi laughed. "*Really*? She'll go home bilingual then!"

I assumed she was joking, but Titi taught Sheopatra Spanish the whole week. She even forced her to order food by herself when we went out to eat. I'm certain that if we'd stayed two weeks longer, Sheopatra would've left the island a fluent Spanish speaker.

The trip was magical. We drove through jungles, jumped into waterfalls, and ate *mofongo* until I was blue in the face. I reconnected with my homeland, the origin of my family's history, and with family members I hadn't seen in years. My family loved Sheo. Titi Paola adored her. Still, Titi had a few reservations about her lesbian niece. She never made us feel unwanted or uncomfortable, but I sensed that her religious beliefs and upbringing were tickling her subconscious.

One night, we met some of my cousins at a strip of bars and restaurants in Ponce. Because it was a weekday, the nightlife was desolate. We were one of only five groups present, but we didn't care. After strolling along the strip and taking in the ocean views nearby, we drank, sang, and salsa-danced until our feet ached, and then we grabbed a late-night dinner.

Boisterous conversations flew across the table of nine. Sheo and I sat on the right side of Titi Paola, who was at the head of the table. She mingled and joked with my older cousin to her left while Sheo and I talked. I'm not sure what the conversation was about, but I know for a fact it wasn't romantic. I believe it had to do with the events of the day and all the fun we'd experienced. Regardless, I felt myself getting closer to Sheo to hear her better, and then closer just because. As the space between us disappeared, so did the music, the people, and the hunger in our stomachs. All I saw were her eyes—her sweet, hazel-green eyes above her stunning smile.

PDA isn't usually our style anyway, but we'd agreed to rein it in even more during our trip out of respect for Titi. Still, I'm not sure if our actions counted as PDA. We weren't kissing or hugging. Our limbs didn't touch. We were leaning over the table on folded elbows, delivering undivided attention to each other. We also fell into fits of schoolgirl giggles from time to time. The energy was obvious.

After the last string of giggles, my cousin began a side conversation with Sheo, and my eyes met Titi Paola's. She was already staring. Her hand clasped mine on the table.

"You guys love each other a lot," Titi whispered. "I can tell. It's beautiful to see. Keep that. Never forget that love. Take care of each other."

To avoid collapsing into her lap, this time with happy sobs, I kept my response short and to the point: "Thank you, Titi. I do love her. She makes me happy."

Day seven arrived in the blink of an eye. We'd filled our tummies with island favorites, our bodies were riddled with mosquito bites my island relatives didn't seem to share, our skin was colored by sun-kissed shades of brown, and our spirits had been recharged by a rest rooted in tranquility and resetting. One successful trip to Puerto Rico—check!

The next morning, my aunt would drive us to the airport where we'd board a plane back to LA and return to our normal lives. But for that last night, as the sun descended behind the mountains, the three of us collected on Titi's porch. We sipped Medalla beers and talked about anything and everything.

"I've really enjoyed you girls," Titi said. "Please come visit me anytime. You guys have a home here."

Our hearts gushed, and we thanked her repeatedly.

Then Titi turned toward Sheo and said, "I am so glad I met you."

"Aw, Titi Paola! I'm so glad I met *you*! Thank you again for allowing us to stay with you."

"You know," Titi began, "when Yoyi said she was bringing a Black girl with her, I didn't think you'd be *so* pretty. You're *so* beautiful, mama."

Record scratch. Hold the phone. What did Titi just say? The week had been perfect. Things couldn't have gone better. And what was Sheo—my activist, bearer-of-Black-pride girlfriend—going to reply? The porch swirled under my feet. Thousands of outcomes played in my mind, thousands of ways the fire would spread, as my thumb twitched near my phone in my pocket, eager to google last-minute hotels we might need to stay in for the night.

While I dove head-first into a pessimistic black hole, Sheo paused for a brief second and then flashed a smile. "Black women are pretty, Titi. Black people are pretty."

"Oh yes, of course... I know... It's just that you are so beautiful, and such a nice young lady."

"Thank you." She released light-hearted, polite laughter. "I get it from my momma!"

They shared a laugh, and the conversation moved on. My limbs took five minutes to thaw. There was a long list of family members I'd expect a comment like that from, but Titi Paola was light-years away from that list. And yet, she'd swept the rug from under my feet when I swore I was standing on tile.

"Baby, it's okay. Really," Sheo said later that night when we were alone and I was on my tenth apology. "Baby, Titi is great. She battled her faith because of her love for you, for us. She's as sweet as pie. But..."

"But why would she say something like that?" I asked.

"Because she's from a different generation, baby. That doesn't excuse it. It's still wrong. All I'm saying is that she's doing the best she can, and I love her no matter what. I love all your family. I love you."

CHAPTER 29

Two Words

Putting one foot in front of the other, I stumbled to the center of the living room. The third Angry Orchard cider was creeping into my limbs.

"Your turn, Yoe!"

A friend handed me a phone with blocks of red and green on the screen.

"I thought we were playing Heads Up!?"

"We are, but it's Black-themed!"

Heads Up! is a phone game where one player has to guess the word displayed on the screen. That player places the phone against their forehead with the screen facing the rest of the players in the room. For example, if the word was pterodactyl, everyone would mimic flying and make dinosaur screeches until the player guessed the right word, like in charades.

Instead of typical categories, like animals or nineties movies, this category was all Black everything, including Black actors, singers, musicians, TV shows, and films.

During my turn, I correctly guessed two words out of

eight—*two words* during the minute-and-a-half-long round. How in the hell did I lose so hard? I glanced down at the screen to review the words I failed to come up with.

The first was *Martin*, the show with Martin Lawrence. I knew of the show but had never watched it growing up.

Next was Lynn Whitfield. After a Google search, I discovered I'd seen her in *Cheetah Girls* and *Madea's Family Reunion*, but I never knew her name.

Then it was *The Players Club*. For this one, someone had said, "A movie about a strip club!"

"*Magic Mike*?" I guessed.

"Wrong. *Magic Mike* isn't a Black movie."

Next was Vivica A. Fox. During this round, everyone kept mentioning *Set It Off*, the movie about four women robbing a bank.

I screamed "Queen Latifah!" and "Jada Pinkett!" until I was hoarse. I didn't know the names of the other actresses in the film.

And last was The Isley Brothers. (After a much-needed introduction, they became one of my favorite bands.)

The two answers I got right were the Wayans Brothers, "the two brothers that make funny movies and include their whole family," and Aaliyah, "the singer that passed away in a devastating plane crash."

I never expected such a loss, but in retrospect, I should've known. Papi is of African descent. Dark-brown chocolate drapes every inch of his skin. He is Black; I am half Black. We are Afro-Latino, Latinos of African descent, but we are not African-*American*.

I grew up in a Latino household. On Saturday mornings, my mother played Héctor Lavoe and Willie Colón while she cleaned the living room. Sheopatra's mom played Marvin Gaye and Anita Baker. I watched *La Rosa de Guadalupe.* Sheopatra watched *The Parkers.* Classic Black films like *Friday* and *Set It Off* were introduced to me by my high-school girlfriend, Tominique. My love for baked macaroni and cheese and collard greens didn't blossom until she served them to me. Because of Tominique and other teenage friends, I knew about bits and pieces of Black culture, but it was still not *my* culture.

I really thought I was going to crush that game into dust, but I'm not African American.

CHAPTER 30

Magic

She could regurgitate every count of choreography with little to no effort. Attentive and laser-focused, she never glazed over the details. She picked up every single angle, direction, and body placement in the choreography. Okay, I'm embellishing the story a bit; she did ace the choreography, but it wasn't terribly difficult.

The kids in the class ranged from age five to seven, so the routines didn't surpass rhythmic step-claps, *chassés*, kicks, and—if I was really pushing the difficulty—a single pirouette.

For most children that age, the goals are basic music comprehension, flexibility, coordination, and beginning technique. Many of the children struggled but would most likely find it in their own time. Not her, though. For her, the basics were a walk in the park. LeAndra was a natural-born dancer.

Most children in that age group are still working on listening skills. Their minds wander. They'll report every detail of their lives, like what they ate for breakfast or what their best friend's name is. I often had to wrangle their drifting trains of thought back into dance steps with a "5, 6, 7, 8." But focus was never an issue for LeAndra. At the beginning of every class, she was the first dancer with her jazz shoes on, standing in her assigned spot on the dance floor. She retained choreography after learning it one or two times while others needed four or five attempts to get it right.

Not only did she learn faster than the rest of the class, but she was also patient. She'd repeat the steps again and again as the other students caught up. Sometimes, quick learners grow impatient while relearning things they already know; it may cause them to become bored, act out, and misbehave. Some children, like myself back in the day, waste no moment of freedom when the teacher is occupied. Side conversations would erupt the second my teacher turned to give a student one-on-one help. But each time I was catering to another student, I'd look up to find LeAndra watching and waiting.

During the first class of the season, we began with basic exercises so that I could assess the level of the dancers. Simple exercises like "step, clap, step, clap" help sharpen the dancers' coordination with movement and music: Step on the one, clap on the two. Step on the three, clap on the four. At the beginning, ripples of steps and claps—instead of one step or clap at a time—vibrated throughout the room. I had faith, though. After a couple of classes, we'd all move to the same beat.

As claps spread around the room like popcorn, something caught my eye: LeAndra's dark-brown hands were clapping on the same beat as mine. Hmm, I thought. Let's switch it up. I leveled up the rhythm: Step, clap, clap. Step, clap, clap. She kept up. For the next ten minutes, I increased the rhythmic and technical difficulty of the exercises, adding in kicks, small leaps, and turns, waiting to see if she'd falter. She nailed every single exercise.

LeAndra was one of the star students for the rest of the year. I even spoke to the studio director about moving her up to the seven-to-nine-year-old class because I was confident she could keep up. In fact, she was already surpassing a few of the children in the older class. Before LeAndra, I'd never been that close to a child prodigy. YouTube videos showcase talented dancers all day, but I'd never personally witnessed the natural, innate, pure talent of someone so young. LeAndra was it.

Talk about Black girl magic.

CHAPTER 31

Crema

J oe Arroyo sang through the speakers. The smell of *carne asada* and *chimichurri* filled the living room. People were dancing, their feet shuffling to the steps of salsa; the rhythm pouring from their hips oozed Colombian *sabor*, flavor. Besides Papi, his adopted brother, Beto, and Papi's girlfriend, Jessica, I didn't know a soul at this party. But Lord, was it fun.

Dressed in formfitting dresses and high heels, Jessica's sisters scurried throughout the house completing all sorts of tasks: cleaning, cooking, setting the table, making drinks, you name it. My eyes widened at the sight of so many women at work like this. At functions with my mother's side of the family, often only one woman was designated for these tasks, and it was usually Mita.

My grandmother would cook, clean, and watch from a distance as the party flourished. Mami might help set up, but once the party started, she freed herself of all host duties. As long as guests knew the whereabouts of the food, drinks, and restroom, all was well. Mami didn't find it necessary to serve the men plates of food, and she preferred to scoop empty bottles into plastic bags the next morning instead of collecting them as the night went on. Having to clean up would've impeded her own partying.

These women were different. Beads of sweat piled near their edges from all the party errands.

"Wipe this up."

"Serve this man a plate."

"Remove that pan from the oven."

"Wash the dishes."

The list went on and on. Their stations were either the kitchen or whatever space in the house needed to be cleaned, while the men remained on the dance floor, playing dominoes, or drinking beer. It intrigued me. I'd never seen Mami take on the role these women chose. I observed, straddling both awe and disbelief.

Jessica's five sisters and two nieces, all of whom Papi hosted during their visit from Colombia, made up the majority of the female cleaning crew. I hadn't met any of Jessica's family prior to that night, and when I arrived at the party, I was stunned.

The doorbell rang twice before a gorgeous, mocha-toned older woman opened the door.

"Hola, soy la hija de Antonio. Mucho gusto," I said. *Hi, I'm Antonio's daughter. Nice to meet you.*

I formally kissed the woman on the cheek, and a smile spread across her face.

"Hola, mi amor! Soy la hermana de Jessica." *Hi, my love! I'm Jessica's sister.*

Though I was smiling, I couldn't control my neck retracting backward. "Hermana?" *Sister?*

"Por supuesto, pero soy un poco mayor." *Of course, but I'm a little older.* She winked before bursting into laughter that made me laugh, too.

Inch by inch, I took in her chocolate skin, full lips, and the freckles sprinkled over her cheeks. I shot a glance at Sheo to my right, whose expression was blank yet pleasant due to the language barrier.

"Nunca sabía que tenía una hermana!" I admitted. *I never knew she had a sister!*

"Hermanas," she corrected. "Somos cinco." *There's five of us.*

I turned to Sheo and said, "This is Jessica's *sister*," and Sheo flashed me a knowing look.

Before I'd taken ten steps into the home, I'd greeted four more Black women of various and beautiful shades—all Jessica's sisters. Her nieces, the daughters of her older sisters, mimicked their facial features to a tee and shared the same dark-mocha complexion. With each family member I met, the shock settled more and more: Jessica was Black. Because of her fair complexion and bone-straight hair, I hadn't had the slightest idea.

After kissing the last sister on the cheek, I examined Papi's girlfriend: full lips, wide nose, wide hips. And when I focused on her hairline, I noticed tight 4C roots spiraling in the Florida humidity. That was new growth, not yet treated by harsh straightening chemicals. I stood in the doorway, bewildered. Jessica was passing, but her sisters gave the truth away: they were Afro-Colombian.

Sheopatra joked in privacy, "Jessica was fooling me with that relaxer, but she can't hide with them sisters! I should've known!" We were gobbling loads of Colombian food in the corner of the living room, away from the rest of the party. "No, seriously though. I can't believe I didn't sense it! I tend to know my people when I see 'em!"

"I've been bamboozled!" I snorted, rice launching from my mouth.

In half an hour, we were washing our food down with cold beers and shots of *aguardiente*, bringing dinner to a close. After Papi connected his phone to the speaker, sounds from Fruko y Sus Tesos soared through the house, and in no time, bodies filled the dance floor. Sheo and I sat back in awe. Through the lens of professional dance, we compared the rhythms of Colombian salsa and Mami's Puerto Rican style.

After I'd shared a dance with my dad, Sheo noted how smooth his style was compared to Roberto's Cuban flair. She said Papi's moves were controlled, suave, and tranquil. Though Papi's steps were more difficult, he wasn't pressed; he wasn't even breaking a sweat. Meanwhile, Roberto was showing off his expertise with level changes, strenuous footwork, and flashy rhythm. He exerted himself so much that steam was coming off his head.

One of Jessica's nieces, who was around my age, took the empty seat beside me. Her eyes sparkled when she looked at me, most likely because Papi perpetually flaunted my dance career. Unconcerned with my broken Spanish, she asked me question after question. And despite my constant fumbling, I enjoyed talking to her. She was a breath of fresh air compared to the older Spanish people. They're often impressed by my career for five seconds before asking when I plan to re-enroll in college. Perhaps it was her youth or her open perspective, but she didn't care about school or what was next. She inquired about the present, the now.

At one point, while showing me a picture on her phone, she said in Spanish, "This is a cream I buy in Colombia. It's expensive, but I think it might be cheaper here. Do you know where I can find it?"

An unfamiliar orange bottle with the word "Crema" on it stared back at me.

"Nunca había visto esto, pero puedo buscarlo el Internet." *I've never seen this bottle before, but I can search for it on the internet.*

After a few seconds, orange bottles filled my phone screen. Not only did I find the cream, but a body soap was available as well. There were tons of package deals on Amazon where she could purchase five bottles for the price of four.

"Dios mío," she said. "Es tan barato! Aqui, tres botellas es el precio de una en Colombia." *My God. It's so cheap! Here, three bottles are the price of one in Colombia.*

"En serio? Deberías comprar varias y venderlas cuando regreses." *Really? You should buy a lot and sell it when you go back.*

Her jaw dropped and her eyes flickered as if a lightbulb had turned on in her head. Moments later, she had added over fifty bottles to her online shopping cart and purchased them. They were scheduled to arrive at my dad's house in two days.

Hell, after she told me how much she'd profit, I made a mental note to take a couple of bottles with me the next time I found myself in Colombia.

As the hours passed, salsa music was replaced with slow, sing-along ballads. Though I knew none of the songs, the show unfolding before me provided plenty of entertainment. People were belting out the lyrics as if they were onstage. Men engaged in bromance-filled side hugs were swaying to the music. And then there were the children, partying in their own world as they ran between the adults with different toys in hand.

My gaze stopped at Jessica's niece. She was swaying with one of her aunts, singing at the top of her lungs. During their karaoke session, the living room light illuminated her face, highlighting something I hadn't noticed before: her skin was flawless! There wasn't a pimple or bump in sight, just smooth melanin spread along her facial features. What in the world?

I unlocked my phone, this time more intrigued by the cream she wanted so badly. I wondered if it was a face or body lotion. If this cream had anything to do with that blemish-free skin of hers, I needed to order some right away. I'd endured grand tussles with acne when I was younger, and a few disrespectful pimples still assaulted my face from time to time. This magic cream must be the secret to getting rid of them!

I swiped through the Amazon listing, pausing at the description to learn more about this potion. When I read it, each word shot me in the chest. It was a skin-bleaching cream.

I'd helped her buy bleaching cream, over fifty bottles of it to be used by her and sold to other Black-Colombian women. My chair swam in the spinning living room.

Through online research, I learned that some women use bleaching cream to lift dark spots and correct hyperpigmentation, but I'm not sure that was the case here. There are more than enough remedies for those ailments that don't lighten skin.

After recovering from my mental crisis, I took a third look at Jessica's niece. Her family members were varying shades of brown, but out of all of them, she was the darkest, teetering toward Papi's color. Were all of them avid users of the cream, or just her?

Latinos, especially those in my parents' generation, love to rant and rave about how those in their home countries don't see color. Racism is an American issue, *their* problem. But those same people who cast judgment on America fail to turn inward. These Latinos don't realize that something as simple as a Black-Colombian girl wanting to lighten her skin *is* racism. It's colorism born from the remnants of slavery and held in place by European standards of beauty—the Whiter, the better.

CHAPTER 32

Put the Wine in the Trunk

T he three of us hurtled down Highway 101 with the sounds of Drake and laughter riddling the air. My attention turned to Sheo's best friend, India, in the backseat as we fired drunken banter at one another: jokes that made no sense, song lyrics that were impeccably incorrect, slurs attached to the ends of our words, and giggles nestled in the spaces. Between all the rum-and-cokes India had ordered at the club and all the Carlo Rossi wine I'd chugged, we were two drunk peas in a pod.

Because I was three months away from my twenty-first birthday, my party ritual included gulping mouthfuls of wine before entering the club and after reuniting with the car. Once I arrived at the vehicle, I retrieved the bottle from the trunk and sipped on it while Sheo smoked a Black & Mild cigar with India. They stood outside the car, leaning against the hood. Since my feet were throbbing from all my dance moves, I remained swaddled in the passenger seat, sipping my wine and contributing to their conversation from the window.

"Friend! Nooo you didn't!" India said.

I love watching their interactions. With their tea-spilling, constant bickering, and playful yet gifted singing, they're two of the most entertaining best friends I've ever seen. Their pet name for one another is especially touching: friend. Its meaning can be determined based on how they emphasize it.

Disbelief? "Friend?!"

Gossip?

With darting eyes, in a hushed whisper, "Friend..."

A playful fight?

With a smirk and an eye roll, "Now, friend..."

This one word that perpetually replaces their real names is laced with so many meanings.

Once they'd finished smoking, India handed her keys to Sheopatra, our designated driver for the night (and most nights). Outside of an occasional Angry Orchard cider, Sheo doesn't drink. At a young age, she quickly learned that alcohol, regardless of the type or amount, doesn't react well with her stomach. I used to think she exaggerated this sensitivity —that is, until I witnessed her vomiting into a toilet because of one margarita. Her stomach is so fickle that I often wonder if she's allergic to alcohol.

I couldn't imagine that life for me, but Sheo doesn't mind. She never enjoyed drinking anyway. She says it makes her feel out of control, so she sticks to weed and tobacco. For her, nightlife indulgence is nothing more than a blunt and a Black & Mild.

Sheo and India piled back into the car as I swallowed my last sip, giving the drink a break until we made it back home. Too lazy to put the bottle back in the trunk, where California law says it should be, I slipped the bottle to India, who tucked it under the passenger seat.

As we barreled down the streets, India and I carried on with our drunken banter while Sheo focused on the road ahead, eager to arrive at our next destination. I knew that the crispy buffalo wings she'd ordered online from NoHo Pizza and Wings were calling her name.

We pulled into the parking lot, and Sheo went in. After returning to the driver's seat, she placed the wings on my lap. "Y'all can just PayPal me."

"Okay," we slurred.

"Fifteen minutes away from the crib. Yes!" Sheo cheered after checking the GPS.

India exhaled. It looked like the night, the rum, and the long drive from Downtown LA to San Fernando Valley were catching up with her. "Friend, I'm just gonna take a nap. Wake me up when we get to the house."

"Okay, boo!" Sheo said. "I'm just gonna eat one wing before we leave. I'm starving!"

In the two minutes it took for Sheopatra to devour a flat, sauce-covered wing, India had laid out in the back seat and was snoring softly.

"Wow, she is *out*." Sheo chuckled. "Let's go."

With a slow and steady pace, she pulled onto the road. I scrolled through song after song in search of the perfect soundtrack for our ride home as a breeze blew through our lowered windows. It was two o'clock in the morning, and we were the only ones on the road. Stillness permeated the air instead of the usual buzz of the North Hollywood streets. In the car, we were silent as well. My search ended at Sade's

"Ordinary Love," a flawless song to round out a successful night on the town.

I paused before hitting the play button. As Sheo crossed an intersection, a faint ring echoed through the air—a sharp, high-pitched ring. The ringing became louder and louder, sirens whirring in the distance. Sheo slowed the car so that we could scan our surroundings. The second she glanced into the rearview mirror, she saw an older compact Toyota turn onto the street about two hundred feet behind us. The car cut the corner so quickly that the back tires skidded over the pavement, causing the vehicle to fishtail. Just as the car straightened, Sheo witnessed two police cruisers turn the corner in the same fashion. The sirens were piercing our ears now. She couldn't believe the scene unfolding in the mirror.

"Is this a high-speed chase?" she asked. She pulled the car to the right side of the road.

What did she see? I wondered. I looked at her, our eyes connecting for a millisecond, and then—

My body lunged forward, my neck struggling to catch up. Materials from the car cracked all around us. The impact had thrown my glasses off, but I could see a blurred outline of Sheo's body thrashing in the driver's seat. Her right arm repeatedly banged against the middle console between us. I screamed before closing my eyes and burying my face in my hands. It felt like the flailing lasted for ages. Then a final impact stopped our momentum. Whatever hit us from the back had forced us to crash into something else.

I lifted my head from my hands, but I couldn't see anything but blurred swirls of lights and fragmented car pieces. Panic set in.

"I can't see! My glasses! Where are my glasses?!" My

hands patted the nearest surfaces as Sheopatra groaned next to me.

"Friend..." India grumbled.

We turned to find India with her head under the driver's seat and her feet in the air, inches away from the roof. The impact had knocked her unbuckled, sleeping body around like a rag doll.

We were all disoriented until our thoughts settled on the same thing: "The wine!" we said in sync. "Where's the wine?! Put the wine in the trunk!"

India wiggled out from under the seat, grabbed what was left of my Carlo Rossi bottle, and tossed it into the trunk behind her. She winced, touching the top of her forehead. She was bleeding profusely from her hairline.

"Friend... My head... Friend, what happened, friend?" She held her head in her hands.

"Are y'all okay?!" Sheo hollered, clutching her right shoulder. I saw flashbacks of her colliding with the console.

"I'm okay," I said. Tears were streaming down my face.

"Friend..."

Before I could say anything else, a flashlight pierced my eyes.

"Ma'am, are you okay?" said a police officer standing in front of the passenger door.

I unbuckled my seatbelt and stepped out of the car with uneasy knees. When I attempted to stand up, a throbbing pain in the lower left side of my back forced me back down. Hunched over, I said, "Yes."

I glanced back at India's Prius. The trunk was flattened into the backseat, and the front of the car had disappeared into the curb we crashed into. The hood was crumpled up to the two front wheels, which were bent in half.

A second officer, who had already opened the door to speak to India, called for an ambulance. A third officer was making his way to Sheo's door.

"Ma'am, can I ask you some questions?" the police officer asked me.

"Yes, of course."

"Well, first, are you okay? Would you like me to call you an ambulance?"

In my head, I replaced the word "ambulance" with "substantial debt." A simple drive to the hospital could easily rack up a five-hundred-dollar bill. My pockets crumbled at the mere thought of it.

Pulsing aches rattled my lower back, but at least I could still walk across the street and order a ten-dollar Uber to the hospital. Same for Sheopatra—she'd been clutching her shoulder since the crash, but she could still move it. There was no blood or protruding bones; therefore, we decided we could safely and cheaply deliver ourselves to the emergency room. However, India's case was different. Blood continued to pour from her head, so the officers wasted no time in calling an ambulance for her.

"Ma'am," the officer repeated, snapping me out of my money-saving trance.

"Yes?"

"Would you like me to call an ambulance for you?"

"No, I'm fine."

He glanced at the hand clutching my lower back. "Um, okay."

A few feet ahead of us, I noticed a young man and

woman propped against a metal gate, handcuffed. To their left was an old Toyota Camry that had slammed into a tree.

"You guys stopped the chase," he said. "After he rear-ended you, he lost control and ran into that tree."

The dots connected. That's what Sheo meant; it really was a high-speed chase.

"Oh, I'm sorry." I'm not sure why an apology was the first thing to leave my mouth. "I had... no clue... it was a chase. Everything happened so fast."

The officer stiffened. "But you heard the sirens, right? Why didn't the driver pull over?"

"By the time... we heard the sirens... and what direction they came from, we were hit."

"But you *did* hear the sirens, right? Sirens mean you should pull over for emergency vehicles to pass. Why didn't you all pull over?"

"We heard the sirens in the distance, but we couldn't tell what direction they were coming from. By the time my girl-friend started pulling over, it was too late."

"So, you're saying you heard the sirens?"

"Yes." Fear struck my nerves. Why did he keep asking that?

He scribbled in his notepad. "Good." I couldn't ignore the condescending sting in his voice.

Before I could reply, a pair of hands gently squeezed my shoulders, bringing my shaking body to a halt. I hadn't noticed how much my body had been violently trembling. Sheo reached in her pocket and placed thick glasses in my hand.

"Are you okay, baby?" she asked.

"Yes, my nerves are just bad. Is India okay?"

"Yeah, they're gonna take her the hospital to run some tests. Her head was bleeding pretty badly. They gave me the name of the hospital, so we can meet her there."

"Maybe we should get checked out, too." I motioned toward her hurt shoulder.

"Sounds like a plan."

Besides some muscle tension, inflammation, minor slipped discs, and India's residual migraines, we walked away intact. However, I still suffer from post-traumatic stress from that car accident. Tasks I had taken for granted, such as driving at night or sleeping in the car, plague me with anxiety.

In the past, I rode carefree during nights out with Sheo as the designated driver. Now, my eyes dart from side to side and all over the road, especially if I've had a few drinks. Anytime a detail from that awful night is repeated, I'm crippled by anxiety and my knees go weak.

With all the events of that night—the accident, the injuries, and the totaled car—there's another thing I'll never forget: "Put the wine in the trunk." The sinking feeling when I realized the alcohol wasn't in its legal place. The fear that consumed me because I was afraid that although the accident wasn't our fault, the police might conjure up a way to blame us.

I've read the stories and seen the viral footage of dirty cops planting drugs on Black people or unnecessarily escalating a situation. Common sense tells me that all cops aren't like that, but fear overwhelms me.

I'm not sure what India and Sheopatra were thinking at that moment, but I was 100 percent sure that if the officers discovered the wine or smelled alcohol on our breath, they would no longer treat us like the victims. Somehow, they would've concluded that being rear-ended by a car trying to evade the police was *our* fault. Somehow, they'd find a reason to haul us to jail. Then, DUI arrests and expenses uncovered by insurance would follow.

Perhaps I had allowed my nerves to dictate my thoughts. But the unfortunate truth was that I didn't fully trust the people who were supposed to protect and serve. Upon impact, I wasn't worried about the well-being of my friends or the ache in my lower back. I had tunnel vision for the wine: "Put the wine in the trunk."

CHAPTER 33

Hey Black!

"Negra! Que lo que hay?" *Black! What's up?*
"Negro, ven aqui!" *Black, come here!*
"Ay mi Negrita bella." *My beautiful little Black girl.*

I 've heard all kinds of Latinos—Black, White, and everything in between—say these words. Pre-Woke Yoe, still unsure whether she was Black, saw no issues with this. *Negro* and *Negra* were terms of endearment; at least, that's what the adults said. They were nicknames. They didn't carry the same meaning as the N-word. Woke Yoe, now neck-deep in her Black discovery, cringes.

They say this new generation does too much. We challenge everything, we change names and labels, and we cancel everything. We're problematic, and these days it's hard to keep up with what you can say and do without being offensive; at least, that's what people say.

I've always considered myself to be half and half; one side of me is rooted in older values while the other half is open to learning new ways. I still believe in a slap on the tush to rear a child, but I'll also respect someone's preferred pronouns and will gladly use an all-gender restroom. If I don't understand something, a little research is more than enough to broaden my views. And even if I don't agree with some new idea, I'll still respect it.

At first, "Woke" Yoe stood firmly in the beliefs that had been instilled in her, like the idea that there's nothing wrong with the nickname *Negra* or *Negro*. I've heard Mami greet someone with "Oye, Negro!" But I've also heard someone call to her, "Hola, Blanca!"

We often use other characteristics as names as well: *Flaca*, skinny; *Gordo*, fat; *Blanca*, white; and *Enano*, midget. These are all nicknames I've heard Latinos use throughout my life. Any characteristic, flaw, or quirk is free game. One of my aunts still calls her daughter *Gorda* to this day.

"Gorda! Donde estas?" *Fat! Where are you?*

"Gorda! Te quiero!" *Fat! I love you!*

Meanwhile, my cousin's round childhood belly and cheeks are long gone. Even though she wears a size 6 now, the nickname remains. That's just the way it is.

I held on to my stance for quite a long time. But as the years passed, there was a shift. I don't know why, but eventually, my eyes narrowed more and more each time I heard a White Latino use *Negro* as a nickname. It felt endearing when Afro-Latinos said it to one another, but I couldn't shake the bad feeling in my chest when non-Black Latinos uttered the word.

As strange as it may sound to someone outside the culture, some non-Black Latinos nickname each other *Negro* or *Negra*. If Fulana has a naturally deep tan and she's standing alongside her olive-skinned family, some family members might call her *Negra* even though there isn't a bit of African DNA to be found. I'd heard it and cocked my head in confusion, but I still held no firm opinion on it—until one day.

I'd scrolled to a Facebook post from one of my childhood friends that featured her four-month-old baby boy. His round, doughy eyes met mine through the screen, and his pin-straight hair was slicked to one side. A crooked, miniature bow tie sat on top of his button-up shirt, like he was a grown man ready for a Sunday fun day. His eyes and light-tan complexion were almost identical to my friend's.

I scrolled through each picture until the post ended, finishing with the caption: "Four months! How did we get here?! I love you, *mi Negrito bello*, my beautiful little Black boy."

I blinked a few times, expecting the words to morph into something else. Images of my friend and the father of her baby flooded my mind: Puerto Rican and Colombian, naturally tan skin, long, straight hair. And their parents had the same features. Maybe Indigenous genes flow through their DNA, but they aren't Black. My friend isn't Black. The father of her child isn't Black. Their baby isn't Black. Why would she call him *Negrito*? Furthermore, why would she feel comfortable doing so on Facebook?

That was the moment that I hopped, skipped, and jumped straight out of neutrality. I had to board the boat with my "problematic" generation on this one. She said, "I love you." She said he was beautiful. Nothing but love exuded from her post, but I couldn't shake the discomfort I felt seeing her refer to her non-Black child as a "beautiful Black boy."

It'd been a while since I'd last spoken to her, so I wasn't compelled to address her. Instead, I took a second to digest her words and then scrolled to the next post in my feed. For the following weeks, I ignored all her posts, scrolling with vigor each time I landed on one. I didn't want to rain on her parade of becoming a mother, but at the same time, I couldn't look at her posts without feeling waves of discomfort.

In the fall, my brother-in-law, Charles, came to Los Angeles for a week. He's a professional drummer who lives in Memphis, and he was in town rehearsing for some shows with a Latino artist. One night after he got out of rehearsal, my wife and I met him for drinks.

"Yo, it'd been so long since I'd seen the crew," Charles said. "It was like a big reunion when we saw each other on the first day."

Sheo and I smiled as he filled us in.

"It was amazing," he continued. "I'm not gonna lie, though. When I saw one of the musicians, I got tight for a second."

"What happened?" Sheo asked.

"He opened his arms and said, 'Oye! What's going on, *Negro*?' My whole body tensed. I was like, Is he calling me a n—? Then I had to remember he's Puerto Rican, and it's not like that. It's just weird cause the word is so similar."

"Yeah, it's not like that," I said. "He said it out of love. Latinos do that, but it's still weird."

To my African-American brothers and sisters out there, it *is* weird. You aren't crazy. I can't police my Latino community. I can't send elaborate dissertations to every Puerto Rican in the world. But I'm here to let you know that it's okay to feel uncomfortable with a Latino calling you *Negro*. It's okay to express that. I'm also 99 percent sure they'll try to explain how it's a term of endearment. After listening, it's still okay to reply, "I understand if your other Black friends are comfortable with that. You can use it with them. Just don't use it with me, please." A real friend will understand.

CHAPTER 34

One Drop

The internet is a big place, filled with lots of people and opinions.

It took no time for me to discover the vast amounts of opinions on biracial people, specifically those from the Black-American community. Some continue to hold on to the one-drop rule: one drop of African blood, and you're Black. Others find the rule problematic because of some biracial peoples' ability to pass. Some hand down the verdict on a case-by-case basis; we accept Tracee Ellis Ross but say "I don't know" when it comes to Rashida Jones.

I can see all sides, so it's hard for me to form a definite opinion. I'm half Black by my father, not by my grandparents or earlier generations, so I cannot and will not deny my African genes. However, I'm not treated like a Black woman by society. Out of respect for my sisters, I cannot act like I am, nor can I claim their daily struggles.

At the end of the day, I'm still the easier pill to swallow, the exotic mix, the example when people fetishize us and say, "I wanna have mixed babies." I still deal with issues concerning my race, and I will continue to express those. But I've never been followed around a 7-Eleven by the store owner like my wife has, and I don't think I ever will.

CHAPTER 35

Resident
White-Black Mom

Young dancers and their parents had gathered in the largest room at the studio with their seats arranged in a semicircle. My rear end wiggled in my seat while I listened attentively. Though Mami was attending the meeting as well, I didn't want to miss a single announcement.

At the age of thirteen, competition season and summer vacation were my favorite times of the year. Endless sleepovers at my cousin's house, theme parks, and mall trips filled our summer itinerary. But competition season, from January to April, was a different beast. Each year, the studio owner chose three or four competitions for us to attend. We'd compete with group numbers, trios, duets, and solos, hoping to receive a platinum—the highest adjudication. It would be years before I'd earn my first platinum, but that never curbed my excitement.

Not only did we get to compete with the routines we'd perfected throughout the season, but the events gave us a chance to see what all the other Central Florida studios were working on. The talent offered by my state never ceased to amaze me.

At each competition, I witnessed dancers in the junior category (nine-to-twelve years old) match the technical capabilities of those in the senior category (fifteen-to-eighteen years old). I looked forward to each studio's production number, which included all the members of the studio, from elementary school kids to those in high school—and on special occasions, the stage parents, too!

The themes ranged from Disney movies, like *The Lion King* and *The Little Mermaid*, to hit Broadway shows, such as *Chicago* and *Pippin*. One of my favorite pieces from another studio was a Britney Spears–themed production number. Dancers from each age group were dressed as the pop star from one of her iconic music videos. It began with five-year-old cuties in pigtails doing pirouettes to "Baby One More Time" and ended with teen students dancing to songs from the *Circus* album. As a young Britney fan, my eyes sparkled watching the entire piece. My studio's Gloria Estefan routine was my favorite production piece. We also did a smaller production piece in honor of Whitney Houston the year she passed. Those performances are still among my fondest memories.

Eager to hear the announcements about this upcoming competition season, I sat in the front of the semicircle. Mami congregated with the other dance moms in the back. The studio owner and two primary teachers stood in the middle of our chairs.

"For this year's competition season, we've decided to change the team makeup," the studio owner began. "Instead of our usual blue eyeshadow and red lipstick, we're going with a black-and-white smoky eye." She held up an eyeshadow palette divided into white, gray, and black sections. Then, one of the younger teachers explained the basics of executing the perfect smoky eye, which I wouldn't master until I was well into my adulthood.

Following the tutorial, the studio owner held up a tube of matte lipstick. "This is the team lipstick for this season: Burgundy from CoverGirl. It's fourteen dollars, but it should last the whole season."

Although wealthy Caucasians and Latinos made up most of the studio's population, quite a few of us were still on scholarship programs.

"Wet n Wild has that same color at Walmart for five dollars," Mami mumbled behind me.

The studio owner gestured toward one of the younger students in the company. Her artic-blue eyes lit up as she took a seat in the center of the semicircle. "This is the new company hairstyle, a headband braid from the left to the right," the studio owner said.

I studied the single blond braid woven to the little girl's scalp. It was like a sideways cornrow beginning above her left ear, stretching along her hairline, and ending above the right ear, like a headband. The rest of her hair fell loose.

"We can pull the loose hair into a bun for our ballet numbers and style it however we want for the other pieces: down, ponytail, whatever the other teachers like."

Ballet was the studio owner's department. She held the style near and dear to her heart and was committed to our training. We often performed classical ballets like *Don Quixote* and *La Esmeralda* in pointe shoes, and the studio required dancers to enroll in three or four ballet classes to be eligible for the competition team.

"You see?" She'd wrapped the girl's hair into a quick ballet bun. "Still perfect for our ballet pieces!"

She then announced the competitions we'd be attending and the weekends they fell on. This year, we'd attend four competitions.

After the meeting, a group of mothers circled Maria Barra, one of the other dance moms.

"Ay, Maria. I don't know why she made that the studio hair. I can't braid at all! My girls are gonna need you!" one mother pleaded.

"Maria, I'm going to meet you every morning on competition days," another mom said.

"Well, I guess we'll all have to set appointments with her," Mami announced.

Out of all the parents, only two mothers could execute the headband braid, and Maria was one of them. A few mothers took their daughters to a professional salon before each competition, but most of them sought Maria's free services.

On the Thursday night before our first competition, Maria's house buzzed with dancers and their mothers. One by one, she braided every dancer's hair.

"Oh, thank you, Maria! You're a lifesaver!" one mother said. "I'll go to your hotel room Saturday morning before the small-group category starts so my daughter can get her braid redone."

Competition weekends usually lasted from Friday to Sunday, depending on how many routines we entered, so she wanted to make sure her daughter rocked a fresh braid on stage.

During the car ride home, I asked Mami, "When are Yayi and I gonna get our braids redone?"

"You're not going to, *mija*. You guys don't need to. We'll just wrap it up when you aren't dancing and touch it up with hairspray if needed."

"Oh, okay." I shrugged.

And she wrapped it up, all right. As soon as I got off stage Friday evening, she slapped those durags onto our heads. That night, she secured the durags once again to ensure they didn't fall off while we slept. During breaks and award ceremonies, the durags would go right back on our heads. A few mothers did the same with their daughters' hair using bandanas, but most of the studio lived their fullest wrap-free lives. On their off times, dancers of all ages frolicked through the competition hallways doing cartwheels and jumping on hotel room beds.

In order to cut costs, it was common for mothers and children to share double-bed hotel rooms for the weekend. I grew accustomed to piling on the bed with Mami and Yayi across from a classmate and her mom. Each night, after lots of dancing, giggles, and whatever beer-induced shenanigans Mami and the dance moms were up to, we'd wrap our hair up and go to bed. Our roommate at the time would lay her bare braid on the cotton pillow.

Throughout the weekend, mothers pleaded with Maria, "Do you have time to redo her hair? It looks fuzzy, and hair-spray won't fix it!"

I'd compare Yayi's and my braids to our classmates' hair. Sure enough, as the days passed, everybody's braids slowly unwound, sprouting baby hairs and wispy strands. One little girl was so active off stage that her braid unraveled entirely. They either spent the rest of the weekend dealing with fuzzy braids or begging Maria to fix them. Yet our hair remained threaded to perfection.

By the time the third competition weekend rolled around, the other mothers had noticed.

"Windy, how come the girls' hair always looks good?"

"Yeah, I thought you didn't know how to braid!"

Mami paused and smiled. "Here." She opened her oversize caboodle, searched the bottom, and pulled out a brand-new silky, black durag. On the front of the packaging, there was a picture of a Black man modeling like an R&B singer. "Put this on their heads whenever they aren't on stage. The entire weekend. Use it when they sleep, too."

Their eyes widened. "Where did you buy that?" one mother asked.

"Any beauty supply store in Seminole Heights, Martin Luther King Boulevard, or across Fletcher," Mami said, naming predominantly Black neighborhoods in Tampa. "But if those areas are too far from you, a bandana could get the job done, too."

The moms buzzed in amazement.

Fast-forward to the last competition of the season, where every single dancer—whether she was White, tan, or olive-toned—sported a silky durag or a bandana to keep her braid intact. It's a memory that tickles me to this day: a sea of mostly White children running around a dance competition with durags on.

Moments like this made Mami the unofficially official "White-Black mom." She handed out durags like they were

Halloween candy and offered hair-care tips to any mother struggling with her daughter's curly hair. A lot of girls at my dance studio had curly hair. Although most of these girls had no known Black DNA, some of them had curls tighter than mine sprouting from their heads. Mami was well aware of the trials and tribulations of trying to manage curly hair when one isn't familiar with it, so she'd help mothers in need.

"Use this leave-in conditioner after you wash her hair, section by section," Mami told one mother.

"Windy, I just can't seem to unknot her hair!" the mother said. "The brush won't go through!"

"Detangle it after you wash, or before rinsing the conditioner."

"That makes sense! I've never tried to detangle her hair wet."

"Oh no, never detangle dry hair. It's too hard, and you'll brush out the curl."

In a flash, she'd turned into the studio's curly-hair expert. Had Instagram and TikTok been around, I'm sure Mami would've become a brand ambassador for some company's curly-hair products.

"Here, try a little of this after putting in the leave-in conditioner. It seals my daughters' curls very nicely," she'd say after giving out a sample size of Ampro's protein gel.

I adored Ampro. My entire high school career relied on that thick, dark-brown gel. It flaked to no end, but I didn't mind because the flakes were brown, identical to the color of my hair, instead of the white snowfall produced by other gels.

Every time I say this to Black Americans, they fall over

laughing. Despite my love for it, most of them hated Ampro gel because it bled onto their clothes and made their curls rock hard if they used too much.

I'm now in my mid-twenties, and Yayi's in their early twenties. It's been years since our dance studio days, yet Mami will still get on the phone and tell me how she put someone's mother "up on game" by giving her Ampro gel for her child.

CHAPTER 36

Black Women Aren't Crazy

I got into a lot of problems in high school.
Black girls didn't like me or wanted to
fight me because I was dating all the
Black boys. I never had issues like that on
the island, so I didn't understand what
the problem was.
—*Mami*

Fulano wouldn't let his ex-girlfriend Keisha near his Instagram: no couple photos, no happy-birthday posts, nothing. Social media was for "business" only. During heated discussions, he never thought twice about raising his voice or calling her out of her name. But when that relationship ended and Becky came around, Fulano morphed into another man. Now, he splattered relationship photos all over his profiles with flowery, thought-out captions. Now, he was suddenly able to communicate and maintain his composure during disagreements instead of raising his voice and using profanity.

I've heard Black men put their brothers "on game."

"Spanish girls are where it's at, bro. They don't stress you out like Black girls."

"White girls are just easier to deal with. You can do whatever you want."

I heard a male Black friend rant and rave about how he steers clear of Black women because they have too much "attitude," but he ended up dating the most hotheaded Latina in school. In the end, Fulana delivered the same amount of stress he'd tried so hard to avoid.

I can be looking busted and crusted with tattered, stained sweatpants on, and my hair thrown into a bun or down along my shoulders with frizz beyond belief. I can exit the car, facing away from a Black man. And even then, he'll *still* catcall me. Flirtatiousness will still escape his lips, even though he's unaware of what my face looks like. All he needed to see was light skin and curly hair.

I can be standing in a group of beautiful brown-skinned women, and a fake-conscious man will still approach me, completely ignoring the chocolate women beside me, and say, "How you doin', queen?"

Black women aren't crazy. They aren't angry or jealous, and they don't make things up. Yet some Black men avoid dating Black women with all their might. I've seen it and heard it. Some become entirely different men with their non-Black girlfriends, magically accessing all the emotional maturity that was absent while dating Black women. Some continue to perpetuate stereotypes about Black women being too loud, angry, or ugly. Self-hate is real. Mixed-race fetishization is real.

This doesn't go for all Black men that date outside their race, hence the use of the word "some." But the truth is that ugly men like this, spewing these ugly ideologies, still exist with they *ugly* ass.

I am in no way speaking down on interracial relationships. How could I? I'm the product of one. But I am against the shallow foundations some of these unions are built upon.

"I want mixed babies."

"Black girls do too much."

"White women are easy."

The list goes on and on.

I'm an advocate for authentic love and solid family structures. I praise individuals who research the culture they'll be merging with, who ask themselves the hard questions: Am I ready to parent Black children? Will I ensure that they have equal connections to both sides of their family? Do I find it important that their friend group represents both races, without leaning too heavily toward one side? Do I have what it takes to have "the talk" with them about their history, about how America views them? And, on a lighter note, will I learn how to care for their hair?

In middle school, I knew a girl named Maya. She didn't go to my school, but she rode the same transfer bus that lugged me to the bus station every day. Tons of light-brown freckles covered her face, matching the natural light-brown tone of her hair. Some of the other Black girls on the bus disliked the Afro that Maya wore.

"Damn, you think she would have good hair cause she so light-skinned, but that shit is still nappy."

"I don't why she come out the house with her hair all over her head like that."

This was years before it became common for Black women to go natural again. Relaxed hair was still the craze. I loved Maya's hair, but other things about her confused me. My sheltered, pubescent brain couldn't fathom that Maya was Black when she spoke and dressed like a White girl. She wore high-end name brands and lived in Westchase, a predominantly White suburb of Tampa. She stuck out like a sore thumb in her sea of White friends. I didn't understand it. A lot of the other students didn't either. They nicknamed her "Oreo" because she seemed White on the inside.

My curiosity led me to insensitively ask Maya about her background one afternoon: "You adopted?" (I pray that my inappropriate question doesn't plague Maya's subconscious or identity today.)

She blinked a few times, taken aback by my blunt inquiry. "Um, no. I'm mixed. My mom is White, and my dad is Black."

"Oh! So Oreo is a really good nickname for you since you both!"

A hint of a smile formed in the corner of her mouth.

I continued, "I didn't know there were Black people in Westchase."

"Oh," she stammered. "I live with my mom, but my dad lives in Robles Park."

"Oh shit! Yo daddy from the hood! Can't nobody mess with him!" I joked.

The ghost of a smile expanded to a full flash of teeth. "Ha! I guess not. I don't know, though. I don't talk to that side of my family. My mom says they're ghetto!" Maya snickered.

"Dang. So you don't talk to aunties, uncles, or cousins on your daddy's side?"

"Nope. My mom says I have to stay away from the hood!"

I laughed her response off, unaware at that age of its pestering truth. Half of me wonders whether her father's behavior warranted complete disconnection from his daughter. The other half of me wonders if he did anything at all. Even if he did do something unspeakable, why disconnect Maya from her extended family on that side? Furthermore, why "stay away from the hood"?

I don't mind interracial relationships. But when biracial children grow up without a connection to their Black side, I mind. I understand the desire to move to a White suburb for a more affordable, family-oriented lifestyle, but parents still have a responsibility to their mixed children. If a child is away from their Black family, it becomes the parent's job to seek Black friends and teachers for their children so that they can form a connection to that side of them. I feel the same way about parents raising children of different ethnicities. A Cuban-and-Puerto-Rican kid or an American-and-Filipino child should learn all the ins and outs of their cultures—*both* cultures. It's important for kids to see all sides of themselves.

That's why representation in media is so important. It isn't some ploy constructed by Generation Z. There's power in a little Dominican girl seeing Latinas on TV playing roles other than maids or sexy bombshells. There's power in a little Black boy watching a Black man play a lawyer instead of a thug or a slave.

Parents control the amount of representation and diversity in their child's world. Any parent, not just those with biracial children, should incorporate diversity and representation into their children's lives. As an adult, having the opportunity to peek into other cultures did wonders for my self-understanding. Imagine what it could do for a child.

CHAPTER 37

I Can't Deliver

L iving as a professional dancer is like trying to survive a game of dodgeball. You dodge a couple of balls with consistent industry work and the ability to pay off bills. Then out of the blue, a ball pelts you in the side—a thousand-dollar dentist bill, or a flat tire—while you're waiting four weeks for a music video check.

As with any entrepreneur or freelancer, work fluctuates for dancers. Sometimes, I jump off a commercial job straight into a tour. Other times, weeks pass before I leave my house for an audition or a job. Because of our unsteady lifestyles, many dancers acquire side hustles to help make ends meet. From babysitting to dog-walking to selling merch, I've seen dancers do it all.

I've worked as a go-go dancer in Ontario and driven for Uber all over San Fernando Valley. Now, I work part-time for my brother-in-law's counseling business in Florida, answering phones, scheduling, and verifying insurance. Because of the time difference, I wake up at 6 a.m. Pacific time and work until 1 p.m. or 2 p.m. All my work is virtual, so I can make a quick call or schedule a patient during a rehearsal.

Recently, my friend Crystal and I were introduced to Amazon Flex, a program where you can deliver for Amazon as a freelancer. You set your own schedule and deliver packages using your personal vehicle. Here are some lessons I learned after my first round of deliveries:

Clean up your car so that you have space for all the packages you have to deliver. I had two outdoor chairs and a speaker in my trunk, so I ran out of room quick!

Wear comfortable shoes. I was wearing the flattest shoes in the world.

If your friend is free, take them with you. Sheo organized the packages in the car while I drove, speeding up the delivery times.

Pick delivery times that are during the day.

As the sun set, an eerie feeling came over me. I no longer felt comfortable walking into people's yards and scouring apartment buildings looking for the correct unit. Many homes and complexes had dim lighting. It creeped me out and, as a woman, it most definitely didn't feel safe. From that day on, I decided to only deliver during the day.

The next time I saw Crystal, we discussed our first experiences as Amazon Flex drivers. I told her how scary it felt to deliver at night.

"Girl, I ended up delivering at night and it was creepy!" Crystal said. "I'm Black. I don't wanna walk up to people's homes at night."

"You right, cause people won't care about the bright-blue Amazon vest you have on either," I replied. "You can't do it at night, sis."

Initially, I'd felt that Crystal was in danger because she was delivering at night. But before her reply, I hadn't considered her being a Black woman. Her womanhood and her Blackness were stacked against her, meaning that her blue Amazon vest didn't matter. Trayvon Martin was on a phone call in his neighborhood, and Ahmaud Arbery was jogging. Yet they were still seen as threats.

Crystal continued, "I wanted to have my boyfriend help me deliver, but I couldn't have him walking up to people's homes at night either. At least I'm a girl. I hope people would see that first."

"Oh no, he *most definitely* can't deliver at night."

I was fearful partially because I watched too much *Dateline*. I'd get worried that an axe murderer would hop around the corner, straight out of a scary movie. On top of the *Dateline* axe murderers, Crystal and her boyfriend had to worry about a White man protecting his home because he's threatened by the color of their skin.

CHAPTER 38

I Can't Subscribe

I can't subscribe to Black-trauma films anymore. I just can't do it.

At the beginning of my Black discovery, my goal was to learn as much as possible about Black history. Fury spread through me while reading about redlining and other systematic methods of oppression. I discovered decades-old stories of Black people moving into White neighborhoods and their deeds magically disappearing, or their homes being burned to the ground.

We know the story of Black Wall Street and how it was destroyed, but not many people know that similar cities existed across the country and suffered a similar fate. This isn't opinion. This isn't a shady political commercial exposing all the wrongdoings of an opposing candidate. All across America, there were White mobs attacking Black towns. History holds a multitude of setbacks endured by Black America.

No matter how much it hurt, I never turned away from the truth. No matter how many tears filled my eyes, I never looked away while watching *Roots*. As I was researching all the known victims of lynching, I hurt for our country, but not because of its dark history. Many colonizers bear a questionable history. I hurt because we hadn't fully acknowledged our actions.

Black History Month is like a large, wet Band-Aid with failing adhesive—useless. It's the one month out of the year where I'd repeatedly learn about Harriet Tubman, but they'd fail to teach me about the systematic racism that occurs in our country today. Getting educated about these topics is so uncommon that White people often assume they're fabrications, just Black people living in the past as if we're the ones in chains instead of our ancestors.

I thank God for the internet. It shows the undeniable proof. For example, Black people still have trouble with home appraisals because Black homes are valued far less. It has been proven again and again that after transforming their homes with pictures of White families and White art, the outcome is significantly different. I've read many articles about families all over the country dealing with this kind of discrimination. Imagine if the internet wasn't around to let these families know they aren't alone. Imagine if they only knew people who gaslighted them and questioned their experiences: "Oh, it wasn't about race!"

As heart-wrenching as it was to watch those three men hunt down Ahmaud Arbery, I thank God there was footage to expose his murderers. My heart aches thinking about his mother possibly scrolling past the video of her son's death or seeing it on the news. But I'm also thankful the video was uploaded for the world to see. As a society, we've added a comical twist to aggressive, entitled White people, nicknaming them "Karen" and "Ken." But on a more serious note, I'm thankful their outbursts are caught on video as well. If those videos weren't around, I wonder if people would believe the victims.

At the beginning of this journey, I watched every Black-history film and documentary, from the empowering to the downright depressing. However, with the influx of "Karen" videos, released body-cam footage, and bystander footage capturing the murders of Black bodies, I've realized my mental capacity is limited. I'm thankful that there's proof of these atrocities, but I also wonder whether our society is being desensitized to watching Black people be murdered. These videos circulate so often with little to no warning for viewers.

This has had long-standing effects on me. As years go by, I've noticed my tolerance for Black-trauma films is shrinking. I lasted thirty minutes watching the Netflix series *When They See Us*, which is based on the Central Park Five. Award-winning shows like *Underground* and *Them* gave me goose-bumps all over and lit a fire in my eyes. There's another series called *Women of the Movement*, and one episode is dedicated to Emmett Till's mother and her pivotal role in the fight for civil rights.

It's been the hottest talk on my Instagram and Twitter feeds, yet I cannot bring myself to watch it. Even some older stories, like the heartbreaking death of Emmett Till, make me shed tears as if they were recent.

At this point, I'm in need of a break. I can't subscribe to any additional Black trauma.

CHAPTER 39

Obama

S queals of joy escaped Mami's mouth. Mita gave a round of applause while rocking back and forth in her recliner. The newsfeed on my Myspace profile erupted with status updates and pictures of our new president and first lady.

The song "My President Is Black" went viral on the internet in a matter of hours. The energy around me was vibrant and full of life. America finally had her first Black president. Barack Obama was a beacon of hope for everyone, but the spirit he provided to Black communities across the nation was life-altering—not to mention that his wife, Michelle, was one of the most educated first ladies in history.

This isn't about the Democratic Party. I'm not advocating his political agenda or his decisions while in office. All politics aside, I enjoy reminiscing on the image of a Black man holding one of the most important jobs in the country; it's an image of representation and hope.

History was made on November 4, 2008. But among all the celebrations at home, at school, and online, sadness was stirring in my heart. My eyes watered at the mere thought of Obama being the president. Images of this charming Black man, his wife, and their two kids sent chills down my spine. America finally had her first Black president, but I couldn't bring myself to be happy. My mind was engulfed by thoughts of racist Americans who had shown their true colors during the election year. At only thirteen years old, I was terrified that the president would be assassinated, that a radical opposer would take his life, leaving his family without a husband and father.

After a few months, this anxiety lifted. But looking back, I wish I could've been more present during that historical moment. People talk about where they were the day Obama became president, just like they talk about where they were during 9/11. These two events are like night and day, but they're both moments we will never forget. I just wish my memory of his election day was more cheerful.

CHAPTER 40

Homeless

 One time, I overheard a woman say, "Mixed people are homeless. They're confused and don't know which home to belong to, so they belong to none."

Many people would consider that statement brash, but for some reason, I found it comical. The words hit the center of my chest and caused my neck to lunge forward, just like when the car brakes are tapped a little too hard. My jaw dropped, but I was still smiling. Dang, I thought. How is she gonna do us like that? To avoid being labeled an eavesdropper, I turned my attention elsewhere as giggles creeped up.

There's a piece of undeniable truth in her statement. At some point, most mixed-race people tussle with identity issues. We may feel more connected to one side than the other, or like we're strangers in both worlds. Either we inherited more features from one side, or we're a perfect mix of both, leaving us unable to blend in at either end.

I've seen the same phenomenon occur with people of different ethnicities. Fulano might identify with the Ecuadorian side of his Panamanian-Ecuadorian mix. Fulana might identify with the Jamaican side of her Cuban-Jamaican mix. I used to feel homeless, too: not Puerto Rican enough, not Colombian enough, not American enough. And once I realized I was Black, I rarely felt Black enough either.

I used to identify with my Puerto Rican side more. I've taken many trips to the island, spoken the dialect, and ate the scrumptious food. Mami took on the primary role in raising me while Roberto came in second. There were a few moments where Papi tied with Roberto, but then he'd drop back down to third place. I used to joke that I was Puerto Rican and Cuban rather than Puerto Rican and Colombian. Because I was surrounded by Roberto and his family, I picked up Cuban vernacular. When I meet a Spanish-speaking person, nine times out of ten, they guess that I'm Puerto Rican, Cuban, or Dominican, never Colombian. Perhaps as I continue to delve into my Colombian heritage, I'll pick up those mannerisms or an accent.

I laughed at that woman's statement because being Puerto Rican, Colombian, sometimes Cuban, and American used to be confusing for me. Some people could say my full name right, but most fumbled through every one of my names except my middle name, Shantell. People understood bits and pieces of me but never the whole thing. Some groups viewed me as part of their own; others didn't. Some of my Puerto Rican family didn't see my father's genes in me. Therefore, they didn't think twice about speaking down on Black people in my presence.

"Black people are dangerous."

"Black people are dirty."

"Black people are gang members."

Other family members saw nothing *but* Papi's genes, so they spewed comments about my sister's looks like uncontrollable vomit.

"What is wrong with your hair? Why does it stand up like that? That has to be Antonio in there."

"Oh, honey, you're lucky you didn't come out your father's color."

"Stay out of the sun so you don't end up like your father."

The constant back and forth left me baffled.

Because I was raised in the States, unlike my parents, there are nuances of their cultures that I'll never be able to access. No matter how fluent I become, my cousins on the island will still say my accent sounds like a *gringa*. No matter how many trips I take to my parents' home countries, it will not erase my American upbringing. It will never amount to the experiences of a native. That feeling used to overwhelm me. Because I wasn't raised in Colombia or Puerto Rico, there would always be a part of me that was empty, vacant of those unique childhood memories and stories.

As I grew older, I thought more about this void and realized it isn't a void at all. It's a space filled with experiences my parents could never have because these experiences are unique to an American upbringing. Later in their lives, my parents ping-ponged from the Spanish-speaking world to the English-speaking world; I was born into the English-speaking world.

From a young age, I knew that Jamaicans, Haitians, and West Africans were our cousins in the kitchen. If I find myself in an unfamiliar place where Puerto Rican food is scarce, I know they'll have rice, beans, and plantains on the menu for me. During one of my last trips to Tampa, I brought a jerk-shrimp plate to my grandmother's house for her to try. She loved it. Though Jamaican food was unfamiliar to her taste buds, its similarity to Puerto Rican cuisine blew her away.

The space in my parents that is filled with memories of Puerto Rico and Colombia is filled with White-American, African-American, and first-generation culture in me. It's filled with rap music, Taylor Swift, and Daddy Yankee. My palate is used to collard greens, hamburgers, and *pollo guisado*. This space isn't a void vacant of Latinidad—it's a melting pot of all the cultures that were vital to my upbringing.

I'm not homeless. I have multiple homes in all kinds of places. I am so blessed.

Acknowledgments

While interviewing Papi for this book, I asked him a lot of questions: How did you meet Mami? How did you meet the Apolinario family? How was your relationship with Mita?

He asked me, "Por qué haces todas estas preguntas? De qué se trata tu libro?" *Why are you asking all these questions? What is your book about?*

I laughed and replied, "I know this is going to sound weird, but for the longest time, I didn't know I was Black. It didn't click until I was about seventeen years old."

"Como?! Soy Negro! Estas ciega?" he joked. *How?! I'm Black! Are you blind?*

"I don't know! I always thought you were just Colombian. And I don't have your color, so I was confused."

"Eres amarilla. No eres blanquita como tu mamá y no eres oscuro como yo. Qué pasa cuando le pones leche al café? Se pone clarito." *You're yellow. You aren't White like your mom, and you aren't dark like me. What happens when you put milk in coffee? It gets lighter.*

* * *

Why did I write a whole book? A book about a little bit of this, a little bit of that, but overall, a book about everything Black. Why?

Believe it or not, this book started out as a script about a story from Mami's childhood. Remember when the greatest dad in the world, Kikin Renovales, left her? Little Windy was so over Mita that she ran to the balcony to call for help because her mother fed her rice with eggs, or "poor people food," every day. That is one of my favorite stories.

When the pandemic began and I had a lot of time on my hands, I wanted to devote more energy to my projects. My wife has a crazy talent for creating. She can think of an award-winning movement visual on a random car ride to 7-Eleven. She's naturally gifted. For some reason, it has always been more difficult for me to create a visual concept, so I wanted to practice that skill. In hopes of creating a short film, I began writing a script about Mami's story. I soon realized three things:

1. It was a global pandemic. Even if I finished the script, I couldn't film it anytime soon.
2. Writing a script is hard.
3. Writing a script is %@*#$!& *hard*!

I stopped writing the script, but I kept jotting down random stories from my childhood and Mami's. While reminiscing, I noted some confusing situations that'd stuck with me the most, ones that made me think. During this time, I revisited many memories, big and small. Somewhere between that period of reflection and the modern-day civil rights movement, this book was born.

I really told inquiring kids, "No, I'm not Black." Papi really used to say, "I'm not Black; I'm Colombian." I thought my hair was difficult and unruly. I had no idea the texture of my hair was beautiful. I didn't know my African side was responsible for the texture of my hair. I just assumed I wasn't as perfect as the rest of my Puerto Rican family. I thought my skin was strange because it wasn't light like my mother's. If Afro-Latinidad had been celebrated or at least discussed during my upbringing, maybe I wouldn't have been so confused. Perhaps it wouldn't have taken twenty years to accept the natural state of my hair, or to learn that the term *pelo malo* is quite offensive. This book was therapeutic for me, helping me make sense of all these thoughts.

Though I feel terrible about how many lives were lost during the COVID-19 pandemic, I'm grateful for the way the pandemic slowed the world down. My industry came to a screeching halt, which forced me to take time off. I used to have trouble sitting still and appreciating God's blessings, but I've since learned to practice gratitude for what I have. I used to be away from my wife way too often. I tumbled through most of my days, adhering to other people's schedules. Now, I strive to prioritize the most important things in life and spend my time with intention.

When I was a kid, I loved writing short stories, and in college, English courses were my favorite. I always loved to tell stories, but never in a million years did I think I'd write a book!

So here I am, a whole Puerto Rican, Colombian, somewhat Cuban (I love you, Roberto!), Black, White, and Latina author. Thank you all for reading my story. Thank you for taking a ride on my journey. If you're a friend, family member, or acquaintance, thank you for being a part of my life! I appreciate and love y'all!

Special thanks goes to:

- Joia-Jordan Symone Johnson.
- Larry Doby Johnson.
- Chazz Cooks.
- Alex Cooks and Tuty.
- The Brumley family.
- My family: Apolinario, Renovales, Gutierrez, and Bejarano.
- The Council.
- Those tirelessly fighting for social justice in this country.
- Bianca Brewton for inspiring me to buckle down and finish what I'd started.
- Sheopatra Streeter-Renovales for always answering questions like "Does this even make sense?" and "What's another word for...?" You are my rock. I love you.

Sneak Peek of my Upcoming Book

So You Wanna Move to LA

Coming in 2023!

There I was, high as a kite at a celebrity's house on the night of my initiation. After three lines of cocaine, I knew a wild night was ahead.

By around 2 a.m., my head was dangling from my neck. It felt like pins and needles ran through my fingers, and images and colors were blurred. That's when the Crips arrived. Unfortunately, my initiation ceremony was interrupted when a group of Bloods showed up and sprayed the whole mansion with gunfire. A bullet pierced my leg in the frenzy. When I woke up in the hospital a few days later, I found out that the doctors couldn't save my leg. But I was still able to complete the initiation ceremony. Call me gang affiliated!

The story I just told never happened and, by the grace of God, never will. I've never used cocaine, nor am I a Crip. But according to my family and friends, drug addiction and gang activity would be my inevitable fate upon moving to Los Angeles.

Now, they never said this outright; instead, these worries were interwoven with the advice and LA "facts" they felt compelled to give me.

"Be careful with that cocaine stuff. It's really big out there!"

"Be careful with the gangs! Don't wear red and blue!"

One of my dance teachers said, "Just please be careful. I don't want you to become a drug addict!"

I nodded and smiled, appearing to take in the advice. But on the inside, I was releasing ear-piercing screams. I wondered how they knew so much about a city they'd never lived in. I learned not to do drugs in my adolescence. I managed to dodge gang life, too. I wanted nothing more than my definition of sound advice: things that could help me with the move, like money management, navigating the industry, and apartment living. I wish someone had warned me about the inflated cost of living. No one told me gas would be about two dollars higher than in my hometown of Tampa, Florida. No one predicted that the rent for a one-bedroom apartment in Van Nuys would equal my sister's mortgage for her brand-new three-bedroom house in Tampa.

I met people who openly used cocaine and other drugs. Some nights, gunshots were a part of my neighborhood's soundtrack. But those experiences didn't affect me as much as the time I sent $1,400 to a fraud landlord. No advice could salvage the terrible car insurance I purchased that didn't cover a dollar on a fender bender.

My loved ones had good intentions. Their concerns were valid. Drug abuse and gang activity are real issues in LA County. Within five minutes of driving into Downtown LA, you'll likely spot a homeless person who's under the influence, mentally ill, or both, talking to themselves or yelling at an aggressor you can't see. Over the past six years, I've noticed an increasing number of homeless people in San Fernando Valley, where I live. When I used to take the bus and train to get around, I'd have to walk through areas with large homeless populations. My steps would quicken, and my eyes would focus on the sidewalk or road ahead of me. I'd step lightly around the miniature tent cities, careful not to draw attention to myself.

The entertainment industry and drugs are very good golf buddies, but I hadn't attended a tournament. In my six years of living here, I also haven't experienced a Bloods-versus-Crips brawl, but I'm sure it's possible. My loved ones' advice sat uneasy with me not because it was false; I was uncomfortable because of what they chose to fixate on.

They were adamant on educating me on the risks of drugs but fell silent when it came to the skills I needed to survive in a new city. Few offered wisdom on renting an apartment, building credit, managing money, or purchasing a car. I was young, so I hadn't hit those milestones yet.

* * *

My name is Yoe Apolinario. I am a professional dancer based out of Los Angeles, California. Since I moved from my hometown of Tampa, FL, in 2015, I've had the opportunity to work with artists like Chris Brown, H.E.R., Taylor Swift, the Backstreet Boys, and more. I've danced behind artists in music videos and on tours. My career has granted me the opportunity to travel extensively, visiting locations as varied as Singapore and Austin, Texas. I'm considered one of the lucky ones. I moved out here with about $5000 in savings. About four months later, I booked my first tour and was able to save even more money.

Years later, I booked one of the biggest tours of my career, allowing me to purchase a townhome in the expensive LA housing market. I never had to get a regular job; by "regular," I mean a 9-to-5 office or service job. By the grace of God, all my side hustles have been flexible and compatible with the ever-changing schedule of a professional dancer. That's rare out here in these streets. On paper, my life in LA looks like nothing short of a dream, and in many ways, it has been. It probably looks easy and free of hardship, as if everything was given to me. Boy, is that not the case.

I describe LA as an eternal roller coaster; emotions, finances, health—it takes them all on a ride. Damn, was it hard. It's *still* hard. I wish somebody would've warned me about a fraction of the things I would experience out here. From apartment hunting to navigating the industry to shopping on a budget, I wish I'd had some sort of guidance. In addition to hard-core adulting, I also had to learn how to navigate the world of celebrities and musical artists before being fired on jobs. That's why I'm writing this book for any reader who wants to make the move to La La Land, for any reader that wants to pursue a career in professional dance or the entertainment industry, and for any reader that wants to move to a big city and become the new fish in the huge pond.

This book will include real-life experiences from my career, and some real names will be used. Whether you want to learn more about my line of work, hear celebrity stories, or know what it's like to live in a big city, you'll find something to relate to in these pages.

About the Author

Yoe Apolinario is a Tampa, Florida native, but currently resides in Los Angeles, California. Most of her days are spent working as a professional movement artist, dancing behind artists in music videos, concerts, and commercials. During free time she's usually loving on her wife and pets, or reacquainting herself with one of her first loves, writing.

Sign up to her newsletter to keep up with new releases!
    yoeapolinario.com

facebook.com/yoeapolinariooo

twitter.com/yoe_apolinario

tiktok.com/@yoe.apolinario

www.ingramcontent.com/pod-product-compliance
Lightning Source LLC
Chambersburg PA
CBHW022046020426
42335CB00012B/572